DATE DUE

WITHDRAWN

Gurus and Oracles

Gurus and Oracles

The Marketing of Information

Miklos Sarvary

The MIT Press
Cambridge, Massachusetts
London, England

MIT Press books may be purchased at special quantity discounts for business or sales promotional use. For information, please email special_sales@mitpress.mit.edu or write to Special Sales Department, The MIT Press, 55 Hayward Street, Cambridge, MA 02142.

This book was set in Sabon by Graphic Composition, Inc., Bogart, Georgia. Printed and bound in the United States of America.

Library of Congress Cataloging-in-Publication Data

Sarvary, M. (Miklos)
Gurus and oracles : the marketing of information / Miklos Sarvary.
    p.   cm.
Includes bibliographical references and index.
ISBN 978-0-262-01694-0 (hbk. : alk. paper)
1. Information services industry. 2. Information networks. 3. Information technology.
I. Title.
HD9999.I492S28   2012
001.068'8—dc23
2011023271

10 9 8 7 6 5 4 3 2 1

Contents

Introduction: The Information Industry

Pigeons, Computers, and Human Networks

In 1850, a young entrepreneur called Paul Julius Reuter started to use carrier pigeons to relay stock market news across a seventy-six-mile gap in the telegraph line between Brussels and Aachen, in neighboring Germany.[1] Reuter's competitive advantage was speed: carrier pigeons beat the train by seven hours. While the concept was simple the details of the implementation were remarkably sophisticated. Reuter used over two hundred pigeons to ensure extra capacity in case unexpected news would require it. In other words, he was worried about proper bandwidth and network availability. He also backed up each news item, sending multiple pigeons with the same message, implementing maybe the first information network to achieve fault tolerance through redundancy. Reuter instituted controls for accuracy and secrecy to ensure reliability and exclusivity of information for his clients. Finally, he also implemented impartial distribution of information, making sure that all news reached clients at the same time. As the telegraph line closed between Aachen and Brussels, pigeons gave way to horses. Over the next century and a half, horses were replaced by telegraph lines, followed by radio broadcast, leased telephone lines, cable, and satellites. Similarly, printed messages gave way to Morse code, digital communication, intelligent terminals, and multimedia output. All these years the news service Reuters, named after Paul J. Reuter, remained one of the world's top information providers.

Roughly one hundred and fifty years after Reuter's carrier pigeons left Aachen, Larry Page and Sergey Brin, two PhD students from Stanford University, launched Google, a new search engine for the World Wide Web. It was based on a new algorithm called PageRank.[2] Google was born in an environment very different from that of Reuter. In a century and a half, information technology had transformed the world so that virtually all people of the planet were connected through vast physical networks capable of transporting any form of information in a matter of seconds. Moreover, beyond easy access of information, the World Wide Web created an environment where information could be *added* to the network just as easily by anyone. In the flood of available data, Page and Brin's goal was to help people identify the information relevant to their needs. PageRank was a vast improvement on existing search algorithms. It was based on the simple idea that a webpage that is referenced by many other pages is likely to be more important than a similar page with fewer incoming reference links. Five years after launch, PageRank made Google the dominant Internet search engine and today one of the largest technology companies of the world.

As a last example, consider McKinsey & Co., a privately held management consulting firm that was born in 1926, almost exactly in the middle of Reuters' and Google's birthdates. It was founded by James McKinsey, a professor at the University of Chicago. In the 1930s Marvin Bower, a young Harvard MBA, transformed the firm to a first-class management consulting partnership, which over the next decades grew to a global professional service firm selling expertise to Fortune 500 companies all over the world. Compared to Google and Reuters, McKinsey is not a technology company using vast networks of computers and complex mathematical algorithms. Rather, it is a "human network" made up of individual consultants who "trade" their knowledge and experience across the world. For more than eighty years, McKinsey & Co. has remained one of the premier management consulting firms.

What is common to these three companies beyond their lasting success? They actually belong to the same industry, the *information industry*. Like Reuters and Google, McKinsey & Co. is essentially an information or knowledge provider. This book is about the universe of similar companies, organizations, or individuals whose core business is to "sell" information to decision makers. A few prominent examples are listed in table 0.1.

The information industry is larger and broader than it seems. In 2010, "business information" alone accounted for about $358 billion worth of sales with over two hundred providers.[3] Some of these companies' business consists of collecting and selling data (this is the case of Reuters or credit rating agencies), while others sell market analysis (e.g., market research firms, financial analysts, or macroeconomic forecasters). There are companies that use their complex expertise to generate customized business strategies for their clients (e.g., management consultants). Part of the media also belongs to the information industry: newspapers and

Table 0.1
Examples of well-known information sellers

Firm	Type/sector	Year founded	Annual revenues: 2009 in $million	Approx. number of employees in 2009
Thomson Reuters Inc.[a]	Global information and news provider	1850	12,948	55,000
Bloomberg LP[b]	Global financial news provider	1981	6,900	11,000
Forrester Research, Inc.[a]	Provider of market research on IT	1983	233	947
Gartner, Inc.[a]	Provider of research and analysis on IT	1979	1,140	4,305
Google Inc.[c]	Internet search engine	1998	23,650	21,805
Reed Elsevier[a]	Publisher and online information provider	1903	9,644	32,300
McKinsey & Co.	Global management-consulting	1926	6,000[d]	17,000[e]
Moody's Corp.[a]	Credit ratings, research and risk analysis	1900	1,797	4,000
Arbitron Inc.[a]	International media and marketing research firm	1949	385	971

[a] 2009 Annual Report. In 2008, Reuters merged with the Thomson Corporation to form Thomson Reuters.
[b] Wikipedia, projected 2010.
[c] Capital IQ.
[d] Wikipedia—2008 Forbes estimate.
[e] Wikipedia—McKinsey & Co. Swiss Office—Key Facts.

news programs on television are clearly in the business of selling information, as are many Internet services that provide online information to the public (e.g., online newspapers, weather forecasting sites, some blogs, or search engines). Even large social media sites such as Facebook, LinkedIn, or Twitter can be considered information vendors as user-generated content becomes a genuine information source for their members. Besides thousands of large corporations, the information industry also includes the millions of small companies and individual experts who make a living selling advice in various domains including finance, accounting, law, engineering, and medicine. Even some doctors who specialize in providing medical diagnoses belong to the information industry.

But why lump these diverse businesses together? A key argument of this book is that they have more in common than it seems. Indeed, information is such a special product that it requires special business practices. But what is so special about information? Before providing an answer, it is important to define exactly what an "information product" is.

Information as a Product

In its "Industry Outlook for 2002," *Business Week* argued that the contribution to the GDP of the "information sector" in the United States was $816 billion.[4] While the figure is in the right range, in its estimate *Business Week* lumped together in the information sector category many unrelated areas including information technology (especially software), the media broadly speaking (films and other content that is mostly for entertainment), and the advertising industry. It even included PC manufacturers and the telecom sector. While all of these categories are related to information in one way or another, these industries have little in common in terms of business issues (consumers' buying behavior, pricing, competition, etc.). Yet common language and the business press usually include these industries in the—so-called—information sector.

The academic literature is a bit more careful in defining the term *information products*. In their seminal book *Information Rules*, Carl Shapiro and Hal Varian define information products as products that can be codified or "digitized."[5] This definition is more precise but still mixes many industries (e.g., music and medical diagnosis) that have little in common other than the (otherwise important) fact that their products can be transported in the form of digital codes. I would like to complement Shapiro and Varian's supply-driven perspective with two additional features that focus on demand.

This book is about information that is used for decision making. This implies that, in our context, the value of information only becomes apparent if we specify the decision that it helps to make. The acquisition (purchase) of information is primarily influenced by the actual background decision for which the information will be an input. We should always keep in mind that when we talk about information as a product, somewhere there is a decision maker struggling to make up his or her mind about something. Therefore, the demand for an information product is the collection of decision makers who can use the information and who are willing to pay for it. Information becomes a product only if it is paid for. Thus, an additional characteristic that we will require for information products is that the decision makers pay for it. In this context, the estimation of demand boils down to the search and analysis of the actual problem that decision makers face.[6] In sum, three characteristics define information products and services:

1. Their core component can be digitized.
2. They are used for decision making.
3. They are paid for by the decision maker.

The information industry consists then of firms producing and selling such products. The companies in table 0.1 are typical examples. However, to really understand the information industry, it is also useful to go through a few counterexamples. First, information products' core component has to be "digitizable." It follows then that an empty computer hard drive, a CD, or a tape are not information products. However, if the core product sold is data that happens to be "packaged" on a computer hard drive or a compact disk, we will obviously consider this "bundle" as an information product as long as the data is used for decision making. Indeed, the second criterion says that only information that is used in decision making qualifies as an information product. For example, movies, music, and the media in general are information (can be easily digitized) but (with the exception of some news) are sold primarily for the purpose of entertainment and, as such, would not be part of the information product category. Finally, we only consider information that is paid for by the buyer (decision maker). An advertisement, for example, would not qualify as an information product. While it is information used for decision making, the decision maker does not pay for it—the advertiser does.

Even though our definition tries to be precise, the boundaries of the information industry are by no means strict. Education, for example, may or may not qualify as an information product. Basic academic subjects such as mathematics or physics qualify more as general tools to sharpen students' minds for later decision making in concrete contexts. A customized executive education program, however, almost qualifies as a consulting service with a potential direct impact on a firm's business decisions. A remaining question of course, is whether such a program can or cannot be digitized. News services have a similar problem fitting in our definition. While they may definitely consist of information useful for decision making (think about a simple weather forecast that guides your weekend plans), many of us look at the evening political news for entertainment rather than for information to use in our decision making. In fact, this dual nature of the news market makes it a special information product that we will discuss in detail in chapter 4. Software is yet another controversial example. While most software products serve a purpose different from decision making, "decision support software" directly aims at helping users make better decisions, is usually paid for by the decision maker, and can easily be digitized.

Another problematic category is "knowledge." We definitely consider knowledge part of the information product category, although there is a big debate among academics whether it can be digitized (codified) or not.[7] Many would argue, for example, that a customized management consulting service cannot be digitized. This is true if one concentrates on the way its final output is generated (e.g., in-depth interviews with corporate executives). However, if we focus on the output of such a service (i.e., the recommendation that it generates) then we can safely talk about knowledge that is readily codified (e.g., summarized in a document or a set of PowerPoint slides). Our requirement that information has to be paid for may generate similar controversy. Based on this criterion, we have argued that advertising is not an information product. We have to acknowledge, however, that the provider of a free information source that generates revenues collected from advertisers easily qualifies as an information seller. Here, as in any standard media revenue model, buyers essentially pay with their attention to information (the ads) that they were not necessarily seeking.

As we will see, these borderline cases stimulate great debate about the major issues that the information industry currently faces. In many ways they will show us how the boundaries of the industry may be pushed further by technological development. For example, high-bandwidth, interactive interfaces are pushing the boundaries of distance learning and have put online education almost at par with traditional face-to-face learning that we traditionally did not consider digitizable. Similarly, the key issues in "knowledge management" all revolve around the questions: can knowledge be codified or not? If so, how? Or think about the problem of extracting value from consumers who are used to free information from public media. It has stimulated the creation of new revenue models in many of today's Internet businesses. We will see that a business that we confidently categorized in traditional industries (maybe even your business) is, in fact, in large part an information business. In sum, our definition of information products shouldn't be seen as a technical constraint but rather as an opportunity to discover a new sector of the economy whose members were previously scattered around in seemingly unrelated industries. The purpose of this book is to explore the evolving universe of these businesses.

Why Study Information Markets?

Some may think that the information industry is very young. To some extent this is true—in the past few decades it has undergone unprecedented growth and change.[8] As in the case of many industries, this growth has largely been fueled by technological breakthroughs. Reuters' success over the last century, for instance, can be easily traced back to its ability to leverage emerging disruptive technologies. Reuters was among the first companies to use radio waves, computer terminals, and other innovations to transmit news across the planet. Currently we are experiencing the continuing development of a new technological platform: the Internet. In front of our eyes, the Internet's most significant application, the World Wide Web, has become a new mass medium with myriad possibilities for information markets. This in itself is a good reason to study the fundamental drivers of the information business.

But the more important reason for our attention to information markets is that they are fascinating and quite different from regular product markets. In the last few decades, research in economics, business strategy, and marketing has shown that information is different from other goods and services. This is especially true in competitive settings and may result in strange competitive-market outcomes. Consider these statements that illustrate this point:

- Unreliable (bad quality) information may be more expensive than reliable (good quality) information even in a competitive market.
- Under some conditions, information sellers may be better off inviting competitors to their market because this may allow them to increase their prices.

• Competition in the market for news may lead to increased media bias but this bias may benefit consumers who would like to discover the truth.
• Consumers may be better off if competing information sellers fix their prices in a cartel.
• Consumers may buy information that they know will never be used.

These statements suggest that information is a peculiar product. While in the last few years academics have started to understand under what circumstances and why this might be the case, there is very little of this wisdom easily accessible to the broader public. Most of it is scattered in hard-to-read scientific journals targeted to isolated academic fields. Even though information constitutes the lifeblood of our economies in many ways, the information industry is still considered to be a marginal and mysterious industry within the services sector. The purpose of this book is to change this perspective and bring some of the recent discoveries about information markets to light. The core question I will try to answer is: what are the implications of these peculiarities for information buyers and sellers? I suggest answers to questions such as:

• What is the information value chain and where should a seller participate in it?
• What new threats and opportunities do recent technological developments present to traditional information companies?
• What is the basis for sustainable competitive advantage for information and knowledge vendors?
• When should we expect dishonesty (bias) from information sellers?
• Why did Google beat all its competitors in the search business?
• What do R&D and production mean in the information industry and what new technologies are available?
• What are prediction markets?

I have written this book for everyone who is interested in answering these questions and is open to the general idea that information markets affect all of us, not just as consumers (decision makers) but maybe even as sellers of information.

The Structure of the Book

The book is divided in two distinct parts. Part I deals with the economics of information. Chapter 1 starts by discussing when a proper market for information can exist. Then, once we have identified these conditions, we follow with an analysis of demand and supply. In chapter 2, we start by describing how people use information in making decisions. In our context, this could be considered as the analysis of "consumer behavior," which constitutes the basis of all demand analysis.

Chapter 3 then explores how firms may respond to the behavior of decision makers. It considers information products that are complements or substitutes (or both), and describes competitive pricing under these two scenarios. We show that the basic properties of information—such as reliability, for instance—have a major *qualitative* impact on how information sellers compete or avoid competition.

Chapter 4 considers distortions in the quality of information: biases and "herding" by information providers. Basically, it explores under what conditions and for what reasons information sellers may lie. An important message of this chapter is that biases may emerge even under competition (sometimes triggered by it) and that these biases may not always make consumers worse off.

Part II of the book concentrates on the problems faced by information sellers and focuses on how to run an information business. What should firms do to create and sell information profitably? It applies the fundamental concepts of strategic analysis to the information industry.

Chapter 5 starts with the analysis of the industry value chain and explores various information-selling formats. Chapter 6 highlights the challenges related to the physical distribution of information and knowledge. This chapter essentially describes the channels (networks, interfaces, and search) that connect information buyers and sellers. These channels have undergone major change in recent years.

Chapter 7 explores how to "brand" information. This chapter deals with communication strategies including activities such as advertising and promotion. Finally, chapter 8 studies the R&D function for information products. It addresses a particularly challenging question: what does R&D mean in the context of information and knowledge? Where should one look for information? What new technologies are available to build knowledge? The book ends with a brief perspective on the history and future of information markets (chapter 9).

I

The Economics of Information

1

Is There a Market for Information?

Imagine the problem of Joe Smith, a young software engineer who, one day, discovers that the mainframe computer of his employer has a fatal design flaw. Being a capable computer scientist, Joe immediately recognizes that his discovery has major consequences and is wondering how to capitalize on it. The options are limitless. He could start by reporting the news to his boss, which could lead to a hefty reward and a promotion, not to mention becoming a hero among his colleagues. He could also report it to the press, seeking broader fame, which would definitely help with his girlfriend. After ditching the idea of blackmail—arguably a risky option—Joe realizes that, instead, he could sell short the mainframe manufacturer's shares on the stock market, then quietly release the news and make a fortune in the process. To do that, however, he needs to open a trading account and get a significant amount of cash. Not knowing much about stock markets and vaguely remembering the legal issues related to insider trading, he decides to call his friend Peter Jones who studied finance and now works as a stockbroker. Joe's plan is to sell Pete his discovery for a hefty sum and let him take care of the details. But what should he charge for the information? How long will it take for the stock to collapse after Pete starts selling? If it takes some time, could he sell the information to another stockbroker as well? After all, by selling it to Pete he still knows what the design flaw is. Also, having known Pete for years, Joe could easily imagine him reselling the information to one of his colleagues anyway. But maybe—thinking along the same lines—Pete will not trust him and will only buy the information for a moderate price.

Joe's headaches related to the valuation and sale of his discovery come from two characteristics of information products well known to economists.[1] As our story illustrates, these two features make information products somewhat unsuitable for sale:

1. Information does not really get "used" (destroyed) when it is "consumed."
2. It is likely to get revealed in its users' actions.

The first characteristic of information means that the consumer of information (the decision maker) can reuse the information again to make other decisions. If these subsequent decisions are numerous then the value of the piece of information that helps make each of them also becomes very high. Under some circumstances, the value of information can be so high to its owner that we may judge owning the information "unfair." This is why insider trading of stocks is forbidden. In our example, Joe got hold of a critical piece of information about the mainframe manufacturer's future losses, which will have a major impact on the firm's stock price. While Joe should certainly be rewarded for his discovery, the reward should be reasonable. On the stock market he can reuse his information in every trade with as many "ignorant" traders as he wants and make a fortune in a very short period of time leading to unreasonable gains. The reasoning is very similar when it is argued that filed patents should expire after a certain time. While we all agree that the inventor of a new technology should reap the benefits of his invention, after a while these benefits should be shared with other members of society.

But the complications stemming from information's indestructible nature do not end here. Joe's other problem is that his friend can resell the information after having used it. Why shouldn't Joe benefit from this sale? This is a general problem in information markets. For another example, consider a client who buys a demand forecast from a market research firm, reads it, and resells it to another client.[2] The producer of the forecast would not be very happy as he now finds himself competing with his own client on the information market. In fact, it is likely that no one would produce forecasts under these conditions. Obviously, the situation is not so bad. Copyright laws ensure that this is considered illegal and that customers doing so can be prosecuted.[3] In fact, this issue is similar to many other industries where reproducing (copying) the product is inexpensive (CDs, DVDs, video cassettes, software, computer games, etc.). As information, all these products are digitizable, making their reproduction cheap. The law makes sure (with more or less success) that proper markets exist for their sale. Nevertheless, most information sellers realize that they are particularly vulnerable in this respect.

In fact, the second characteristic of information—that it gets revealed in consumers' actions—may make the law quite ineffective in protecting the owner of information. Imagine that I want to introduce a new product. I base my decision on the market's potential and I buy a forecast from a respectable market research firm. The forecast says that the demand potential is high and I launch my product. Observing the launch, does a competitor need to buy the same forecast to figure out whether the potential is high or low? Clearly not! He can infer the answer from my decision to go ahead and launch the product. If the problem is serious, potential consumers will be reluctant to buy information and instead will wait for others to make a move first. This incentive to free ride on information purchased by others then would lead to a situation where there would be no demand for information at all. In turn, information sellers (forecasters in this case) would not even exist. Fortunately, for most information markets, the situation is, again, not so bad. The reason is "noise." Our example is simplistic because we assumed that it is enough to observe a firm introducing a product to judge market size. In reality this is not the case. To do so one would need to know all the intricate details of that firm's decision problem, its costs, the product's role in the firm's entire product line, and so on. All these aspects are typically (although not always) unknown to competitors. Furthermore, the time needed for a product's introduction is not trivial so copying a competitor may be much more difficult. There is therefore plenty of scope for information markets.

Nevertheless it is useful to keep in mind the idea that consumers' decisions—if they are revealed in their actions—should reveal the information that these decisions were based on. In some product markets this is a real problem. Which ones are these? Clearly, those where transactions are simple, take little time, and are easily observable and frequent. Again, stock markets are likely candidates and our friend Joe's worries about the time it will take for his target stock price to collapse are not at all unfounded. In stock markets, people decide on a very limited set of actions (sell or buy) and these are highly observable by others. Economists have shown that a "secret" held by a trader (such as the one that Pete is supposed to hold) will be quickly revealed by his/her trading behavior[4]—not the details but certainly the relevant information (e.g., the consequences of the computer's design flaw on the firm's stock price). Therefore, in financial markets information revelation may be a problem for the production of information. In a seminal paper, the famous economists Sanford J. Grossman and Joseph E. Stiglitz show that if *all* information is revealed in traders' behavior, there is no value in buying private information at all.[5] Consequently, since no one wants to buy information, no one has an incentive to produce any information. The result is that such financial markets may be undersupplied with information, which is clearly not optimal for their proper functioning. A market with little information on the fundamentals (demand and supply conditions) is more of a blind betting ground than a thorough price-setting mechanism with the purpose of efficient capital allocation.

The fact that there may be little incentive to produce information is just one consequence of information revelation. Another issue might be that—even if the information exists—there may be little incentive to sell it. Ignoring for a second Joe's nontrivial costs and risk involved in this business, if he only wanted to maximize his revenues from his discovery he should short the stock of the mainframe manufacturer himself instead of selling the information to Pete. This intuition was verified in an article published in 2003 by *The Economist*.[6] It reports the surprising findings of two researchers from Emory University and the University of Illinois at Urbana-Champaign. They analyzed the effect of stock recommendations by equity researchers in various countries for the time period 1993 to 2002. Their conclusion was that, by and large, stock recommendations have no or very little effect on stock prices (with a somewhat better picture in the United States where recommendations may change prices by a few percentage points). The article proposes two explanations. First, it might just be difficult to beat the markets, in other words, the information produced is not of good quality. The second explanation is even more intriguing. Maybe there is good-quality information produced somewhere, but is not for sale. *The Economist* concludes: "It is only those who cannot make money from their research who sell it. The surprise is that there is value in any research at all."

Again, these pessimistic conclusions concern liquid markets with a large number of very simple and visible transactions. In other information markets this effect is far less relevant. In fact, even financial information markets have seen a boom in the last decades thanks to all the market inefficiencies and the "noise" produced by random traders with random goals and objectives.

In sum, consistent with the reality in which information markets flourish, the rest of our discussion assumes the proper functioning of information markets, that is, where ownership can be protected by copyright laws and private information does not get revealed in people's actions. While information sellers need to be aware of their market's potential vulnerability, these market conditions do apply to the vast majority of information products.

If we accept this premise then our next task is to determine the demand and the supply of information. Again, it is useful to refer back to Kenneth Arrow's famous analysis. He argues that information can only be valued in the context of the decision that it helps make. Understanding how information enters people's decision making is crucial for the valuation of information. Therefore, in the chapters that follow, we need to start by looking at the foundations of decision theory.

2

Decisions and Information

A Classic Puzzle: Where Is the Treasure?

Imagine three identical doors. One of them hides a treasure; the other two are doors to empty rooms. The doors are closed and your job is to guess which door hides the treasure. You can open only one door. Without any further information you will randomly point to a door and open it. Your chance of finding the treasure is 1 in 3. Now imagine that a "fairy"—who knows where the treasure is—decides to "help" you. Once you have pointed to a door (but before you have opened it), she opens one of the remaining two doors—always one that *does not* contain the treasure. The question is: are you going to change your original choice? Stop reading here and think about it!

I like puzzles in general but I particularly like this one for two reasons. First, it is very simple, yet it contains all major aspects of a typical decision problem. All decisions consider trade-offs between alternatives (in our case, each door is an alternative). The decision boils down to the choice of a subset of alternatives to the detriment of others. Each alternative usually corresponds to some expected payoff that is earned if the alternative is chosen and foregone if not (in our case, the treasure is the payoff behind one of the doors and nothing is behind the other two). Another crucial aspect of decisions is that they usually include uncertainty. The best choice between the alternatives usually depends on the outcome of some uncertain event that is not under the control of the decision maker. The uncertainty can also be about the payoff amount associated with the alternatives. In our puzzle, the uncertainty is about the whereabouts of the treasure. If there is no uncertainty then the decision is usually trivial.

The second reason why this is a cool riddle is that it clearly shows where the value of information comes in. By now you have probably figured out the answer to the puzzle so let me tell you what it is. The answer is "yes." You should always change your original choice. There are several ways to show this. One of them—the tedious way—consists of calculating for each door the conditional probability that it hides the treasure after the fairy's move. Then, it turns out that this conditional probability is higher for the door that you have not pointed to originally. Intuitively, the argument consists in realizing that in two-thirds of the cases (when you originally pointed to a door without the treasure) the fairy has no real choice but to open the other wrong door. In all these cases you are better off changing your mind. It is only in one-third of the cases (when you originally pointed to the right door) that the fairy has a choice and changing your mind is a mistake.

Yet another way to see the solution is the following. We all agree that the fairy provides you with some useful information—she essentially rules out one of the doors. Now, if you do not change your mind then in no way can you make use of this information. You basically ignore the fairy's statement and in fact, could even choose not to listen to her. Her statement will have no consequence. The only way to incorporate the information provided by the fairy is to do something. But you do not have many choices in this situation. You only have one possible action available: changing your original choice. Thus, you should do so. This is the only possible way to make any use of the information that was provided to you.

Let us generalize the insight of the puzzle. In the context of all decisions, the value of information products comes from reducing the uncertainty associated with the decision. The value can be thought of as the extra expected benefit that the decision maker gets when he or she uses the information to make the decision. But notice that information can only have value if it potentially leads to a different decision from the one that the decision maker would have taken without it. In other words, *information only has value to a decision maker if it has the potential to change his decision.*

This is an important aspect of information products that is often ignored by information sellers and even decision makers. An incredible amount of information is offered and acquired at great cost even though people have already made up their mind about the decision. *Before* the purchase of information, an information buyer should always ask: how will I change my actions if the information says X or Y? For an information vendor, the most important question to ask is: how can my product or service potentially change my customers' minds? Said differently, the more customers believe that the product will deliver a surprise, the more they should see value in it.

We would expect information sellers to communicate to their customers that they are indeed likely to get a surprise. Although this seems obvious, professional information sellers often do not follow this practice. Think, for example, about financial analysts all promoting the same stocks, or high-tech market research firms all writing the same optimistic reports about the computer industry. The popular business press often describes such behavior as "herding." Herding was often blamed for the buildup of the Internet bubble (especially after it burst in 2000) and of the more recent credit bubble. As we will see later in this chapter, just observing that forecasters' predictions are correlated is not necessarily evidence of herding, but it is true that such firms may have strong incentives to report forecasts consistent with the status quo. For example, information providers are typically risk averse and worry about their reputation. They are particularly afraid of recommendations that go against "conventional wisdom." This may make sense if they have a short time horizon. It is always risky to have a controversial opinion. Having a different position raises interest and exposes the forecaster to scrutiny and criticism, so most information offered tends to confirm people's prior beliefs. Is there any value in such information? Of course! It is comforting. But then, the seller needs to realize that she is in the insurance business. If the seller wants to be in the information business, then she should build a reputation for providing information that has the potential to have a real impact on people's decisions.

The exact value of information cannot be calculated without knowing the details of the corresponding decision. You really need to know the alternatives and the trade-offs associated with them. This is an equally important lesson for information sellers. Marketers will preach: "know your customers' needs." In information markets this translates to "*know your customers' decisions.*" While this again seems obvious, my experience indicates that few information companies study the decisions of their customers. A good example is the pricing of industry reports. Most industry research firms will tell you that they price their reports by the size of the report. A big binder on the worldwide cellular market is worth $10,000. The twenty-page summary is worth $500. Pricing information is particularly complex as we will see later. Still, it should always start with a careful analysis of the customer's decision problem. Only after this has been done can other considerations be taken into account.

Information Product Attributes

The value of information does not *only* depend on the characteristics of the decision of course. It is also linked to the characteristics or attributes of the information product itself. Among these the most important one is the *reliability* of information. Reliability is the most basic attribute of every information product. Consumers' choice of information products will always consider this basic feature. The higher the reliability of information, the more valuable it is. What else matters to consumers besides reliability when they purchase information? To answer this question we need to assume that they have a *choice* between multiple information sources.

Like other markets, information markets are competitive, usually with a variety of competing sellers. The decision maker chooses among firms' offerings depending on their products' reliability and price. Every market works this way, doesn't it? Well, maybe not. Does the decision maker really have to make a choice? He has another alternative, namely to buy from multiple information vendors. The benefit is clear: if he combines multiple information sources he may end up with even better information and be able to make a better decision. But there is a cost: paying for multiple products.

That multiple "competing" products can be combined by potential buyers is an important characteristic of the demand for information, and as we will see it makes competition radically different from that in other industries. When does combining multiple information products make sense? The answer depends on how reliable and how *independent* the information sources are. Besides reliability, independence is the second core attribute of information products, although it can only be considered in the context of multiple information products.

The benefit of an independent opinion should be obvious. If buyers can purchase multiple information products, they are more likely to consider the ones that are perceived to be independent from one another. An information seller with a truly independent perspective is more likely to enter buyers' consideration sets. Why purchase several pieces of information if they all say the same thing? Again this sounds quite obvious, but information sellers often seem to forget it and actually do tend to say the same thing. This would be understandable if they were very accurate, but often they aren't; yet they still have correlated opinions. Independence manifests itself by often having different opinions from others. In the short run this is risky. However, if over time the seller can establish a reputation for being an independent source of information, chances are that the seller will not compete with others but rather complement their opinions.

The more a product is independent from competing products the more valuable it is when pooled with them. Independence sounds very much like difference. So are we simply back at the old differentiation story? Not quite. Traditional product differentiation is about making sure that you address a different set of customers (or a different set of needs) than your competitors. Here, the idea is to please the same customer but with a product that adds value by augmenting the quality of other products rather than by replacing them.

Besides reliability and independence there are other information product attributes that may be of value to decision makers. The timeliness of information and its ease of use are also advantages frequently mentioned by information sellers. While these may be important factors and may even represent competitive advantage in certain contexts, they are less fundamental than reliability and independence in shaping competition. In other words, these features of information do not lead to the unusual market outcomes that we will discuss in this chapter.

Information Attributes and Perceptions

Let's accept for now that reliability and independence are the key information product attributes influencing consumers' choice of information providers. But how do people assess reliability or the quality of information? In real life, data rarely exist about the accuracy of information providers. Similarly, how can people assess the independence of different information sources? Where can they find data about these aspects of the market?

To be fair, in a few information product categories there is good data available about reliability. One of these categories is financial analyst reports. In response to the large-scale disappointments after the collapse of the Internet stock market bubble, more and more companies decided to offer ratings on financial analysts. AQ Publication is an example mostly for international markets, and StarMine is its equivalent focusing on the United States. Their data reveal that small analyst boutiques often outperform the well-known investment banks.[1] However, even for these services where such data is available, how objective is it? It is hard to believe that consumers use such data exclusively. It is more likely that they also rely on other peripheral signals such as the analyst's client base to develop perceptions of reliability.

Marketers know that people rarely make decisions based on tangible product attributes. In fact, they would argue that such attributes may not even exist. The abstract dimensions that drive people's choice behaviors are the core subjects of consumer psychology. These include complicated concepts such as "sporty"-ness for cars, "cool"-ness for sunglasses and soft drinks, and "reliability" for industrial items. A simple way to summarize the marketing concept is: "marketing is realizing *and* accepting that only perceptions matter." Thus, the real question is not whether exact measures of probabilities exist and where, but rather where do perceptions of reliability and independence come from in information markets.

Consumers use signals to generate perceptions about complex product attributes. The role of advertising and marketing effort in general is to create such signals. For example, the sound of the click of a ballpoint pen has been shown to be an important cue for evaluating the pen's quality. Similarly, the sound of a car door closing contributes to consumers' perceptions of the overall quality of the car. The weight of a pocket calculator influences users' perceptions of its level of sophistication. In services, the existence of fresh flowers in the lobby has an impact on the evaluation of the service provider. There are many more classic examples. The importance of simple signals generating complex consumer perceptions is no different for information products. The core characteristic that we called reliability is a complex perceived attribute that people infer from market signals.

In information markets, these signals may refer to two different entities. First, they may refer to the firm selling the information. Firms build a "reputation" for quality. Their reputation comes from a number of things. It could come from the prestige of the clients they serve (e.g., top management consultants serve many Fortune 500 companies). It may come from the type of people they employ (e.g., their recruits are from Harvard, the University of Chicago, or MIT). They may have proprietary special technology (e.g., their medical lab or hospital may be better equipped than others). These cues all tell customers something about the information providers' quality. What is common to the cues is that they are all referring to the information seller.

There is a whole set of other cues, however, that will strongly influence the evaluation of the information product's quality but have nothing to do with the provider of information. Remember that the value of information is based on two things: the characteristics of the information and those of the decision problem. Just as for the reliability of information, the consumer's decision problem is also based on perceptions. In particular, how much initial uncertainty the decision maker faces depends on his subjective judgment. If the decision maker believes that uncertainty is low then the value of additional information may be smaller. Think about the market forecast for a new brand in a mature product category (e.g., lawnmowers). If the forecast is done for Germany it is likely to be more accurate than the same forecast produced by the same market research firm with identical methodology but for China. Why? Because the initial uncertainty about the demand may be higher in China than in Germany. In fact, the client may judge that uncertainty is so high that any forecast done with that firm's methodology is meaningless in emerging markets.

Data to form an informed judgment about the business environment is available in real life. Table 2.1 is a good example. It shows cellular subscriber projections in the 1980s as reported by various respectable industry participants, experts, and market research firms. How would a cellular service provider assess the uncertainty of this market by looking at these forecasts and, especially, at their variability? It is easy to see from table 2.1 that research firms' perspectives on the future of mobile telecommunications in the United States were wildly different, sometimes showing differences ten times larger. Compare for example the forecast for the year 1990 of 0.43 million subscribers versus seven million subscribers by the Yankee Group and Arthur Andersen, two well-known analysts at the time. Interestingly, even the same firm came up with significantly different forecasts over time (see the Shosteck Associates 1983 and 1987 reports mentioned in the table). Clearly, chances are that an observer of this industry would have evaluated it as facing high uncertainty and risk. Consequently, even if a research firm had impeccable credentials, any cellular projections sold by this firm would have been evaluated as uncertain (unreliable).

For a more recent example, consider the fluctuation of oil prices between 2007 and 2008. By May 2008, the price of a barrel of oil had climbed to over $120, beating a record every week and essentially doubling compared to the start of 2007. Under these circumstances and because oil is the basis of all economic activity, everyone was interested in knowing what the price was going to be in the next few years. Expert forecasters were at a loss, however. In a 2008 article, *Business Week* reached out to reputed industry experts.[2] Its forecasts ranged from $70 to $200 for 2009 and from $130 to $500 four years out. Clearly, with such a broad range of forecasts, decision makers' perception of uncertainty is going to be high. Irrespective of the reputation of the information providers, they will not perceive the information to be reliable.

Table 2.1
Cellular subscriber projections in the 1980s

Information seller	Date of projection	Population included	Date projected for	Number of subscribers (millions)
Yankee	1985	Total market	1990	0.43
Shosteck Associates	1983	Urban pop.	Potential	0.53
Shosteck Associates[a]	1987	n/a	1995	9–12
A. D. Little	1980	Total market	1990	1
A. D. Little[b]	1985	n/a	1994	3
Cellular business systems	1985	n/a	1993	3.8
BCG	1985	Total likely	1990	1.2
Link Resources	1984	Total market	1990	1.4
EMG	1985	Total market	1990	1.8
Business Comm. Co.[c]	1985	n/a	1993	1.3
Lehman Brothers	1982	Top 90 markets	1989	2
Dean Witter	1982	Total market	1990	2.1
IRD	1980	Total market	Cellular	2.5
RRNA	1985	Total market	1990	2.6
Goldman Group[d]	1988	n/a	2000	9
DLJ	1985	Top 90 markets	1990	2.6
Leigh	1982	Urban pop.	1990	3
Arthur Andersen	1984	Total market	1990	7
AT & T[e]	1985	n/a	2000	30–40
		Actual market	1990	5.2

Sources: Telocator, February 1986, 22–27.
[a] *Telephone Engineer and Management*, July 1987.
[b] *Washington Business Journal*, April 1, 1985.
[c] *New York Times*, June 23, 1985.
[d] *Cellular Business*, January 1988.
[e] *Peoria Illinois Journal Star*, May 26, 1985.

Information marketers have the option of marketing based on the consumers' decision problem rather than on their own product's characteristics. Why is this important? Isn't it more credible to advertise one's own product features? Well, it is relevant because information marketers often need to market the unreliability of their information. I repeat: information marketers can be better off if they tell customers that their product is *not* reliable. To see why, you need to read on for a few more pages. But if you accept this statement for now, then it becomes obvious that it is better to influence customers' perception of reliability by talking about the decision problem than by talking about the inadequate methodology or sources used by the firm. What if Forrester Research said: "Our forecasts are really not that accurate"? This does not sound too good. Instead, Forrester could say: "The technology sector is extremely volatile." Both statements will influence consumers' perception of the accuracy of Forrester's industry reports. The second statement, however, does not destroy the firm's reputation as an information provider. In fact, an article in *The Wall Street Journal* published right after the Internet crash in 2001 illustrates that Forrester did not have any choice but to actively manage consumers' perceptions about the business environment.[3] At the time, the firm was accused of having contributed on many occasions to the "dot.com crash" by providing overly optimistic forecasts on various aspects of the Internet. Forrester needed to "teach" its customers that the domain of its forecasts was highly volatile and, therefore, the accuracy of its forecasts was quite low. While this sounds like a marketing challenge, as we will see later, it may actually help a firm become more profitable.

As with reliability, the relative similarity or independence of information products is also based on perceptions that are in turn generated by market signals. Academic studies show that across a variety of areas (and with large variance) experts' opinions are quite correlated. On a scale from 0 to 1 the average correlation among experts is as high as 0.6. This relatively low level of independence is attributed to a number of objective factors, including common background (e.g., schooling or methodology used), the fact that experts may use similar sources of information (i.e., the same or overlapping data), or that they are averse to having an extreme opinion (they tend to imitate each other). This type of objective study does not exist for most real information product categories, although the financial sector is again an exception. For example, *Global Investor* published a study in 2003 that formally ranked financial analysts on the independence dimension (see table 2.2).[4]

Table 2.2
Providers of the most independent European equity research*

Rank in 2002	Rank in 2001	Research firm	% respondents
1	—	Sanford C. Berstein	15.06%
2	2	Deutsche Bank	8.13%
3	1	UBS Warburg	6.93%
4	—	CSFB	6.63%
5	—	Collins Stewart	6.02%
6	7	HSBC	5.12%
7	—	Crédit Agricole Indosuez	4.22%
8	5	Exane	3.92%
9	10	Fox Pitt Kelton	3.61%
9	3	Lehman Brothers	3.61%

Source: Global Investor, www.globalinvestormagazine.com.
*Ranked by percentage of respondents selecting that firm as most independent

The objectivity of this data is again questionable, but for information products covering other sectors it doesn't even exist. As a result, most of the time, consumers develop relevant perceptions of independence from signals. These signals usually relate to three factors: (1) the school of thought that the information seller belongs to, (2) its methodology or technology (equipment), and (3) the source of data that it is relying on. In medicine for instance, a homeopath's opinion is likely to be perceived as more independent than that of a regular doctor because homeopaths follow a radically different school of thought about human health. A financial analyst using an original model or a separate dataset for forecasting is perceived to be independent from others relying on a traditional method. For marketing strategists it is critical to recognize the power of these and similar signals in shaping consumers' basic perceptions.

Armed with the two key information product attributes—reliability and independence—we now have a rough idea of how consumers acquire information when they are faced with multiple information suppliers. Next, we need to figure out how the suppliers of information will react to consumer perceptions.

The Perceptual Map for Information Products

Marketing strategists have a useful tool for analyzing the competitive landscape: the perceptual map. It is like the map that a general uses

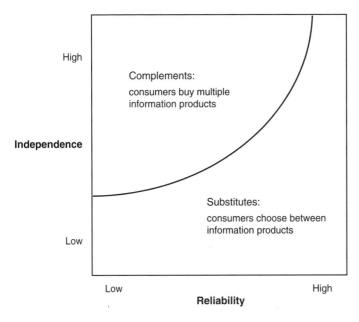

Figure 2.1
The perceptual map for information products

when he places his troops on a battlefield. It shows enemy positions as well as the features of the terrain, which need to be controlled to win the battle. A perceptual map plots competing products in a space defined by the key perceived attributes of the product category. For information products, figure 2.1 represents such a map with the two critical dimensions—reliability and independence—as the main coordinates. One choice factor is still missing from the figure: price. Price is different from the generic product attributes and it usually never figures on perceptual maps. The reason is that price can be changed easily while other product perceptions take a long time to develop or change. Therefore, it is hard to change the position of a product on the map. In our case, it is hard to change consumers' perceptions or beliefs about an information product's reliability or "originality" (independence). Therefore, price is really dictated by the position that the product occupies on the map relative to its competitors. Usually, the more the product is sheltered (isolated) from competitors, the higher the price it can command from customers.

To make the analysis of consumer choice simple, assume that there are only two information sellers and their products have the same characteristics.[5] How will consumers buy information from these two firms? Which product will they choose? Will they buy from both, and when?

Let's start by looking at some extreme cases. Assume first that the two products are both very reliable so their position is somewhere on the extreme right side of the square representing the perceptual space in figure 2.1. Clearly, if the two information sources are reliable then consumers only need a single product to reveal the truth and help them make a correct decision. Since the two products are similar, chances are that consumers' choice will be driven by price. They will buy only one—the cheaper—information product. This is how most products compete with each other. We say that they are *substitutes*.

Now take the case where the two products are highly correlated. Then they are positioned somewhere along the lower side of the square in the figure. High correlation (low independence) means that the two products are likely to say the same thing irrespective of whether it is the truth or not. Again, knowing this, the buyer is likely to purchase only one of the products. Why ask for a second opinion if I expect it to be the same as the first one? The products are substitutes again and consumers' choice will be driven by price, just as in the previous case.

Let us now take the upper-left corner of the perceptual map. Here, the two products have low reliability and are independent from each other. Low reliability means that one product is not likely to be worth much. Independence means however, that if we pool the two firms' opinions together, we will get significantly closer to the truth. The interesting situation here is that individually the products are worth little, but when they are purchased together, suddenly their joint value is high. We call such products *complements*.

We are surrounded with millions of examples of product complements. Think about tennis balls and tennis rackets. The ball is worth little without the racket and vice versa. Although similar examples abound, we rarely imagine two firms "competing" when they sell complements. We usually assume that they are collaborators in the marketplace. This is not quite true but it is certain that they do not compete as harshly as if they sold substitutes. In our example, some consumers may actually be willing to pay double price for two pieces of information to get significantly closer to the truth. In contrast, most consumers may not want to pay the price for a single piece of information if they know that it is too inaccurate to refine their view of the world.

A key insight here is that it is not just independence that makes information products complements. Unreliability also has a role. In fact, its role is even more important. It is the unreliability of information products that creates the need for consulting multiple sources. Independence only makes sure that it is worth doing so. Now, it should be clear why it may be beneficial for information sellers to market their products as unreliable. It means that "competing" products are complements rather than substitutes. Consumers tend to buy multiple products and there is little competition between information sellers.

Do consumers really think and behave the way we described in chapter 1, and do firms price according to the corresponding perceptual map? Evidence from experimental markets as well as data from real information markets suggest that the answer is "yes."

A Simple Experiment

Since information stores are not at every other corner, it is hard to observe people in a clean "information shopping" mode. So, to have clean evidence, I first wanted to observe information purchase behavior in an isolated and controlled environment. With one of my colleagues at Stanford Business School, we ran an experiment in which real decision makers purchased information. First, we needed a decision context. This was easy. At the time, I was running an MBA course in which students had to play a well-known simulation game called INDUSTRAT™.[6] They were in groups and each group (representing a firm) had to compete against all others in a well-defined industry. They had to make decisions about production levels, prices, R&D investment, advertising, sales force size and compensation, and more. In essence they were running their own firm competing against others. They took the job seriously because half of their grade depended on their firm's performance relative to other firms' at the end of the course. The interesting part of the INDUSTRAT game is that the industry has many uncertainties. There is uncertainty about the demand, costs, consumers' preferences, macroeconomic conditions (e.g., inflation), and so on. Each firm can spend part of its profit to buy reports on various topics to reduce the uncertainty that it faces when setting its business policies. In essence, each firm can buy information to guide its decisions.

In this environment, our simple experiment consisted of allowing the groups to purchase information about the industry demand (a crucial parameter for many decisions) from two alternative information sellers (consultants). We manipulated the key attributes of the two information sources, reliability and independence, as well as the price of information. Groups were given some history about the past performance of the consultants based on which they could develop perceptions about their reliability and independence. An example of such an experimental stimulus is provided in figure 2.2.

Figure 2.2 contains two scenarios. In one of them (represented by the top table) the two consultants (A and B) have highly correlated forecasts but their demand forecasts are actually quite accurate: if A underestimates the truth, chances are that B will make the same mistake but this mistake is likely to be small. This is the typical scenario of two information products that are substitutes. In contrast, at the bottom (for a different set of products) two different consultants (1 and 2) are compared with very inaccurate forecasts. However, their opinions are negatively correlated. This is a situation where if one underestimates the demand, the other will likely overestimate it. This case therefore is even better than having independent forecasts. Too bad that in practice this is unlikely to happen. Nevertheless it perfectly represents the situation where the two products are complements: buying one of them is likely to lead to a big mistake, but both of them together are likely to provide an accurate representation of reality. Figure 2.2 is only an example of the situations we have presented to students. In the experiment they were randomly assigned to multiple scenarios. We were interested in the general patterns of choice as a function of these scenarios.

What did we observe? First, we observed that people are careless if the price of information is low relative to their budget: they just buy everything. In marketing terms, in this case, information is a *low-involvement product* and this case is not very interesting. When the cost of information becomes important relative to their budget, the groups become more careful and start paying attention to the history of information sellers. One interesting insight was that the groups were relatively good at interpreting the data (signals) provided to them. In other words, they developed realistic perceptions about the information's reliability and correlatedness across different vendors. This was reflected in their decisions and also confirmed in debriefings that we carried out at the end of the experiment. Most groups purchased one information product when the sources were reliable or correlated, or both. They purchased from both vendors only if these were independent (or negatively correlated) and the information was unreliable. When the consultants' forecasts were correlated or when their reports were generally reliable the groups only spent money on one of the information products. The experiment was repeated many times with different conditions, using various decision makers (students,

History of forecasts by different consultants
(per thousand)

Product name	Demand forecast of		
	Consultant A	Consultant B	True demand
PANNI	132	124	217
JOZSI	475	456	527
ELEK	693	727	636
KINGA	868	810	798
ZSOLT	1012	1050	994

Product name	Demand forecast of		
	Consultant 1	Consultant 2	True demand
ERZSI	12	565	271
TAMAS	669	315	505
HOKEL	798	349	546
ARON	1054	591	834
LUCSA	781	1098	982

Consultants A and B sell demand forecasts for the Korex market, while Consultants 1 and 2 sell demand forecasts for the Lomex market. Each consultant charges **$16,000** for a demand forecast.

Please, circle the firm whose demand forecast you wish to order (you may order from as many firms as you want):

Consultant A $_____

Consultant B $_____

Consultant 1 $_____

Consultant 2 $_____

Total: $_____

Figure 2.2
Stimulus for information purchase experiment

managers, novices versus experts). All the results suggest that (1) people develop roughly correct perceptions about product attributes from available market signals, and (2) they purchase information consistently with these perceptions, following choice patterns that are strikingly different for information products that are substitutes versus complements.

Market Evidence

But can we systematically observe such behavior in real information markets? As I mentioned, it is not easy to identify clean information markets in the first place and systematic empirical evidence is lacking in the area. Nevertheless the answer is "yes"! I have done secondary research for various information product categories to discover how consumers and firms behaved. A good example of an industry where consumers clearly think about competing products as complements is the market research industry that consists of information technology (IT) analyst firms such as the Gartner Group, Forrester Research, Meta Group, and some others. These market research firms help their clients choose between emerging technologies and applications through more or less customized consulting services or reports on competitive and market trends. A few important competitors at the time of the Internet bubble are listed in table 2.3.

In 1997, *Information Week* conducted an exhaustive survey with the customer base of this industry. The survey covered over 300 information systems executives asking for their assessment of IT analysts' services on a variety of dimensions. The results of the survey were written up in an article entitled "Analyzing the Analysts."[7] The data show that in the market of high-tech industry reports, it is more the rule than the exception that clients buy the reports of multiple analysts. The article quotes Forrester, for instance, claiming that 90 percent of its clients are also Gartner's (a competitor's) clients. This is even more interesting because most executives

Table 2.3
Major high-tech analysts by revenue at the end of the Internet bubble

Firm	Approx. 2000 revenues ($millions)
Gartner	1000+
Forrester	150
Meta	120
Yankee	50
Giga	50
Jupiter	30

perceived the price of these industry reports to be quite high. Furthermore, they all complained about the "quality" of the analysts' reports, in terms of reliability.

At first sight this market seems to be strange. Why would people buy multiple versions of expensive, poor-quality products? A bit of reflection helps to make sense of this pattern. The first question to ask is what is meant by low reliability in this market? Are market forecasts in the high-tech sector low quality because firms are incompetent? Not really. The problem is that the high-tech sector is extremely volatile with tons of innovations popping up on a daily basis, each promising attractive applications down the road. The volatility of technology stocks is well known to be high and it correctly reflects the uncertainty of this sector. Thus, the reliability of any forecast—even if it was done by a competent researcher—is likely to be low. At the same time the stakes in the sector are high. Business investors are constantly making large bets on industry trends, emerging standards, and innovations. So the need for information is very high. The problem is that the information products offered cannot be trusted in this uncertain environment. The solution is simple: buy several reports to compare the multiple and possibly diverging perspectives of research firms. Even if one has to pay for pricey reports multiple times it is worth it since millions may be invested in a given technology. Essentially, investors cannot afford not to buy any of the information products and will likely end up buying all of them.

The example of high-tech analysts is similar to the situation that we saw previously with the telecommunication sector in the 1980s (see table 2.1). At that time cellular was the emerging new technology in the industry and large telecom firms were trying to estimate the future prospects of the market. Research firms were keen to fulfill the insatiable demand for information about the future evolution of mobile technology and used a variety of methodologies and data sources to estimate future cellular demand. Notice that most of these forecasters were reputable firms who did not just randomly cook up some forecast. They probably ran surveys or used secondary sources to estimate the future number of subscribers. Yet the numbers tell us that their opinions were wildly divergent. What should a telecom company do in this situation? Who should it listen to? Maybe to all of them! In this environment, who would dare to rely on a single forecast to plan production capacity or to set a marketing budget even a year ahead? Indeed, if one were to take the average of these nineteen forecasts, the number (about 4.8 million) would be within an acceptable range of the actual number of subscribers (5.2 million) calculated with the benefit of hindsight (see table 2.1).

In other words, this information market seems like the perfect case for complementary products where clients buy from multiple sellers. Our suspicion was confirmed. In an interview with one of the senior executives of a consulting firm specialized in selling industry reports on mobile telecom trends, we were told that there was little competition between his firm and other industry forecasters. In fact, he told us that in trade shows and other professional gatherings they used to regularly exchange customer lists—arguably their most important corporate assets. He explained that they knew that customers would purchase all available information about the future of the industry anyway given the high stakes and uncertainty surrounding the future. They never feared losing a customer to another firm with a "better" report. In fact, he told us that besides formal research firms, industry "gurus" also did very well at the time. Their "untraditional" ways of looking at the industry intrigued telecom firms, whose leaders often listened to their recommendations as well.

Key Lessons

1. Information as a commodity is fundamentally different from other products in that (1) it does not get destroyed when it is consumed and (2) it may get revealed in the actions of its consumer (the decision maker). These characteristics of information products make the proper functioning of information markets vulnerable.
2. The value of information is intimately linked to the decision that it helps make. Information only has value if it has the potential to change a decision. An information seller needs to know his customers' decisions.
3. All information products have—at least—three key perceived choice attributes: (1) reliability, (2) independence (from alternative products), and (3) price. Buyers of information will use these attributes to decide on a purchase strategy. Plot your and your competitors' products on the perceptual map defined by reliability and independence to gauge consumers' likely information-purchasing strategies. If information products are unreliable *and* uncorrelated, then buyers may purchase multiple information products.
4. Reliable information products tend to compete as substitutes leading to harsh competition between firms. Unreliable (and uncorrelated) information products compete as complements, leading to mild competition between information sellers.

3

Competitive Pricing of Information

Information Substitutes

How will information sellers react to the consumers' choice patterns described in chapter 2? We have seen that the nature of competition is quite different depending on the information's characteristics. If competing information is accurate or highly correlated, or both, consumers are likely to treat it as a substitute and competition is harsh between vendors. In fact, most product markets are like this. People need only one item from the multiple options that firms offer and they choose the best "value." Value in turn depends on the product's quality and its price. In markets for substitutes competitors tend to undercut each other's prices.

The standard way to avoid harsh competition is to differentiate. The more a firm is differentiated the less harsh is the competition with other firms. Still, differentiation does not completely shelter firms from the effect of a price cut by another firm. If I sell high-quality cars, at the margin, I am still hurt by a price cut in the lower-quality categories. The marginal consumers for whom higher quality just tipped the balance for my product now may be seduced by the really low price of a "value" brand. At the margin this provides an incentive for me (the high-quality seller) to reduce my price as well. When information products are substitutes they tend to follow this same pattern: prices are low and competition is harsh between firms.

Many information products are like this. Take financial information as an example. The price of a stock quote is available from multiple sources. Moreover, all these sources are very reliable so they are likely to say the same thing. No one will pay a high price for a stock quote. This is why during the 1990's Internet bubble, Reuters, Bloomberg, Bridge Information Systems, and other financial information vendors became worried about the explosive growth of the Internet.[1] You might think that the main value proposition of these services is the reliability of information. In fact, they often use this claim as a sales argument. But the truth is, the reliability of their distribution system is what made these services so successful. Financial information vendors' core competence lay in information technology, especially the management of large networks. They provided the high-quality proprietary infrastructure to deliver information that was otherwise quite trivial and accurate. The Internet directly challenged this value proposition. It is a public network, in other words, free of charge. Moreover, during the 1990s, its reliability increased dramatically. By the end of the 1990s, anyone could use it to distribute reliable stock quotes. Internet-based providers of financial information such as Moneyline.com quickly emerged and were joined by existing media firms introducing their own financial information services (e.g., Yahoo!Finance or CNNMoney. com). The market share controlled by these new entrants had reached 14 percent by the end of the 1990s. More entry and virtually identical offerings quickly triggered price competition and traditional financial information vendors were right to be worried. Indeed, prices for most financial information products dropped considerably and many of the traditional players had to go out of business. Dow Jones, for example sold its Telerate business to Bridge Information Systems, which in turn filed for bankruptcy in February 2001 and was ultimately acquired by Reuters later that year.[2]

Information Complements

The competitive landscape looks quite different when firms are selling unreliable information or knowledge and when each of them has a unique, independent perspective. In this case (as we saw in chapter 2) information products are complements and the forces that drive price setting by sellers are strikingly different. Now a decrease in price by one firm triggers higher pricing by the others. Why? Customers want to buy multiple products (remember a single product alone does not have much value) and in terms of price, what is relevant to them is the total price that they pay for the bundled products. If a firm reduces its price for one product, this means that consumers are willing to pay more for the other products in the bundle as long as the total price remains the same. In such an environment, no firm, of course, will decrease prices. Quite the opposite! In their quest to extract as much as possible from the total that consumers are willing to pay for the bundle, firms tend to overprice their own products. This usually results in high prices, which may even scare away some consumers.

Industry practice is consistent with this pricing pattern. Remember the complaints of the customers of high-tech analysts in *Information Week*'s broad survey? They all mention their dissatisfaction with the fact that, despite the low reliability of analyst reports, prices were very high. Well, nothing is strange here! It is precisely because analysts' reports have low reliability that prices can increase. Customers have to buy multiple reports to be confident about their decisions and this pushes information sellers to charge high prices. In the 1990s the case was similar for analysts selling reports for the mobile telecommunication industry: prices were high and there was little competition among sellers.

With such dramatic impact on pricing, it is clear that information sellers should be aware if they sell reliable or unreliable information. The competitive dynamics are strikingly different in the two cases, and without understanding these dynamics it is easy to make mistakes. I had the chance to closely observe a situation where such a mistake was barely avoided. After the Internet boom of the 1990s, many of the high-tech industry specialists (the same firms who were in the survey by *Information Week*) saw a sharp drop in their sales figures. In most companies, such an event immediately triggers a discussion about pricing. High-tech market research firms were no exception and my client immediately thought that there was something wrong with his firm's prices. His argument: "If sales drops maybe this is because our prices are too high and consumers buy competitive products." In fact, he mentioned rumors that competitors did indeed drop their prices for industry reports to respond to the tough economic environment. This logic is not quite true for complements, however. Remember, if consumers buy from one firm, they are also likely to buy from another because they need to compare different perspectives. In fact, when we did a quick market survey, it confirmed that most of the large firms (investment banks, global consulting firms) continued to buy as before. The sales drop largely came from startups facing serious cash shortages and suddenly not having the money to pay for reports at all. Adjusting prices would not have helped these small customers whose research budget essentially fell to zero from one day to the other. But it would have led to significant losses from sales to larger firms whose buying behavior hadn't changed. In information markets, we need to control our usual reflexes concerning pricing. Exploring customers' purchase behaviors in great detail helps develop the right reflexes.

Scientific Evidence: Another Experiment

Although the industry examples I just discussed all seem to be consistent with this strange relationship between information quality and price, they did not satisfy my curiosity about information pricing. Academics are always afraid that what they observe in the real world is just an artifact of the circumstances—especially if their observations are so counterintuitive. Do we really believe that decision makers are so sophisticated as to distinguish between reliable and unreliable information? Can they figure out the optimal buying strategies in both cases? Information sellers are even more suspicious. Do we really believe that firms can see behind consumers' complex information acquisition strategies and price their products accordingly in the face of competition?

To help answer these questions, I decided to examine information markets more thoroughly, in a controlled experiment where alternative explanations could be ruled out.[3] One of my colleagues at INSEAD and I decided to run such an experiment. Remember the experiments we ran at Stanford University selling market forecasts to groups of students running their own firms and competing with each other in a market simulation game? We decided to replicate these experiments with one important modification. As before, we manipulated the reliability (quality) of the information products (market forecasts) that the firms could buy and use for their decisions. For simplicity we set correlation to zero, so all information products were independent. The big difference this time, however, was that we did *not* manipulate price directly. Instead, we gave the information products (forecasts) to information sellers (other groups of students) and told them to set the price of information themselves. In other words, the information sellers were also firms whose performance (and course grades) was measured by how much profit they generated on the information market (again, their grades were linked to their firm's profits). This setup simulated a real market. On one side (the buyer side) we had the firms competing with each other and relying on market forecasts. On the other, seller side we had information sellers who competed with each other to sell information to buyers. We were curious to see if the information buyers' purchase behavior and the information sellers' pricing behavior would replicate the patterns predicted by the theory.

The results were beyond our expectations. They are summarized in figure 3.1, which shows how prices evolved over time (for six decision periods) for the high- and low-quality information products. We were worried that our "novice" information sellers would not be able to figure out the market forces at hand during the few weeks they played the game and that their pricing would reflect broad experimentation. Our worries were not totally unfounded. Indeed, the first few pricing decisions suggested that information sellers did not really understand what was going on and prices were going up and down without any sensible

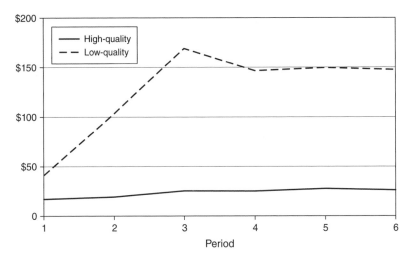

Figure 3.1
Average prices paid by information buyers in experimental market
Source: Christen and Sarvary 2007

pattern (note that in figure 3.1 we only show the average prices across
ten sellers, which tend to increase quite regularly). Debriefings at the end
of the experiment confirmed that the groups were indeed experimenting
with prices. After a few rounds, however, prices stabilized (average prices
flattening out after period 3) and they reflected exactly what we were
expecting: when information sellers competed with reliable (high-quality)
products they had to drop prices because buyers only needed one product and ended up buying from the cheaper seller. Prices dropped so low
that in some of these markets the buyers actually reverted to purchasing
multiple reliable forecasts. The opposite was true when the information
sellers sold unreliable (low-quality) but uncorrelated information. Then,
prices were high—three or four times higher than on the reliable information market—and buyers consistently bought multiple forecasts. We have
repeated the experiment with various modifications, making sure that we
controlled for any alternative explanations. We always found the same
pattern: after some hesitation prices clearly separated, always climbing
significantly higher for unreliable information.[4] It seems that information
markets do function this way.

Complementarity and substitution clearly have a dramatic effect on the
nature of competition between information sellers, at least in a static world
where all information is purchased at once. Indeed, so far, we have only

considered markets where decision makers typically purchase information on a single "shopping trip." Sometimes, however, this is not the case. It can happen that consumers purchase information sequentially over time. In these situations, consumers' willingness to pay for further information may change over time. Next we will explore some of these more complex, dynamic information markets.

Buying a Second Opinion

Imagine that a person has an annoying headache and goes to see a doctor. After some routine examinations, the doctor concludes that she has high blood pressure and recommends a change of lifestyle or a minor cure involving some medication. Most likely she goes home reassured and may even "forget" the doctor's advice concerning lifestyle. Then imagine that instead the doctor diagnoses a major disease that requires serious surgery or a painful treatment. Chances are that under this scenario the person will seek the opinion of a second doctor. It is also likely she will try to find a doctor specializing in the disease. While under the first scenario it did not even cross her mind that further information should be purchased, under the second one she is willing to pay for a second opinion.

Up to this point, we have always assumed that the consumer of information (the decision maker) purchased at one time all the information needed. This makes sense in many contexts. For instance, a consulting firm may purchase several industry reports at the beginning of the year to use them across many assignments on that industry. In fact, it is likely that this firm subscribes to new editions automatically in a contract renewed every year. As the new reports become available its source of information is updated automatically. But often this is not how decision makers acquire information. As in the headache example just cited, the decision maker's need for information often changes as new evidence is revealed to him. Depending on what she learns, she may decide to buy more information or stop buying information all together. When do information buyers behave this way? How should information vendors react to such buying behavior?

What is interesting in this example is that whatever the diagnosis says, the buyer's perception about the information provider's reliability has not changed. Why is the buyer willing to accept one opinion from the seller of information, but questions the other? The answer is quite simple and relates to the concept of what statisticians call "prior information" or simply the "prior."

Decisions can always be made—even if no information has been explicitly acquired. We can always choose between alternatives based on our intuition or based on our existing beliefs, for example. For all practical purposes, such beliefs have to be considered as information too. Their importance depends on how much we believe in them. The strength of such subjective beliefs can be considered the reliability of our prior information.

Thus, new information is always acquired in a context where some prior information already exists about the truth relevant to the decision in question. The new information then needs to be combined with this prior and the correct way of doing this is to weight each (the prior and the new information) with their respective reliabilities. In fact, this is a very general rule—named Bayes' rule after Thomas Bayes of the eighteenth century—for combining information coming from multiple sources (as long as these sources are uncorrelated[5]). So the recipe is: take each source of information (including the prior), weight them with their relative reliabilities, and add them up. This weighted average forecast is going to be the best estimate of the truth. Do people use information sources like this in the real world? There is a big debate about this in psychology, which would be difficult to settle here. The answer is: more or less, yes. There are various anomalies[6] but there is broad evidence that, on average, people are remarkably Bayesian.[7]

Let's get back to our headache example. It is incomplete because we have not made explicit the patient's prior even though it was strongly present. Clearly, that prior was that she had no serious disease. After all, a priori, a minor headache is not the end of the world. On the one hand, when the patient hears that this is indeed what the examination results say, the prior gets confirmed. This is as if two sources said that she was fine: the prior and the doctor. Thus, her confidence in her knowledge about her health is high. On the other hand, when she is told that she has a serious disease her prior is contradicted. This means that she does not know which to believe, her prior or the doctor's diagnosis. In other words, her confidence in her state of knowledge becomes smaller and her willingness to acquire further information becomes high. In fact, the first diagnosis can create such high uncertainty that she is willing to pay more for information the second time.

Pricing First versus Second Opinions

When is sequential purchase of information an important issue, and what will firms do to take it into account in their pricing decisions? First, sequential information gathering usually happens in so-called private information markets, that is, when the information is very specific to the customer and is not produced regularly for a larger market. An industry report produced by Forrester Research about the high-tech sector is useful across many clients and many situations. It is purchased regularly by all interested parties (consulting firms, investment banks, industry players) in anticipation of its use in different situations over the next couple of months. These information products have public value and, for lack of a better word, I will call them *public information goods*.

In contrast, a doctor's diagnosis of a patient's condition is a unique product: the information generated is very specific to one patient. It only has private value: it has been produced specifically for the client and contains information of little value for the rest of the world. Medical diagnosis is a typical private information product. It is also a category where there is an explicit market for second opinions. In fact, such second opinions are often required not just by the patients themselves but also by insurance companies when the diagnosis implies a major treatment. There are well-established statistics about the benefits of such medical second opinion services (see table 3.1).[8]

The value of a medical second opinion has been recently recognized by firms as well. Increasingly, companies have started to offer second opinion benefits to their employees. *Business Week* reported the case of a special provider of such services: Boston-based Best Doctors.[9] The firm consists of a network of medical experts chosen by their peers. They review initial diagnoses and treatment plans. The article claims that when they get involved, they change the diagnosis in about 20 percent of the cases while the recommended treatment is changed 60 percent of the time, thus reducing the treatment cost by tens of thousands of dollars. It is interesting that over 80 percent of the cases consist of some very serious disease (cancer, heart-related, or neurological cases).

But there are other private information markets besides medical diagnosis. A management consulting report produced for a bank to assess its competitive strategy is also private information. It is unlikely that this bank would hire multiple consultants at the same time for the same job.[10] It is possible, however, that after hearing the final recommendation of the management consultant, the bank's management may decide to get a second opinion from another one. I witnessed this situation many times in the former East bloc countries after the fall of the Berlin Wall. Most businesses in the region needed to entirely restructure their operations and consultants often helped them come up with a business strategy.

Table 3.1
Results of mandatory second opinions

Operations proposed		Opposed by second doctor	
Type	Number	Number	Percentage
Varicose vein	6	3	50
Breast	23	9	39
Back	29	11	38
Bunion	22	8	36
Knee	58	16	28
Prostate	17	3	18
Hysterectomy	53	9	17
Gall bladder	25	3	12
Tonsils and adenoids	43	5	12
Dilation and curettage	43	3	7
Cataract	52	3	6
Hernia	39	2	5
Nose	25	1	4
Total	**435**	**76**	**17**

Source: Owens-Illinois Inc. Adapted from "Why Should You Get a Second Opinion?" Reprinted from April 15, 1985, issue of *Business Week* by special permission, copyright © 1985 by The McGraw-Hill Companies, Inc.

I personally observed the case of a major retail bank that hired three management consultants in a row over a two-year period. Each time the consultants came back with their final assessment, the bank management thought that what they suggested was too risky. Each time, a new firm was brought in to provide a second opinion. Second opinion markets are also common for accounting and legal advice, but one can find them in all instances when private information is sold.

How should information sellers take into account their clients' sequential purchase of information? Clearly, if clients' needs and willingness to pay for information changes over time as they consume information, it is important for firms to know whether they are the first ones or the second ones to be approached by potential customers. This would affect their prices and also the perceptions about their products' attributes that they would like to promote. In fact, a proactive firm might want to decide whether or not it wants to sell first or second opinions. The trade-offs are clear. If it sells first opinions chances are that it will sell to a larger market. Most consumers will consider approaching it first. In contrast, if it sells second opinions, then only a subset of the market (those who have been

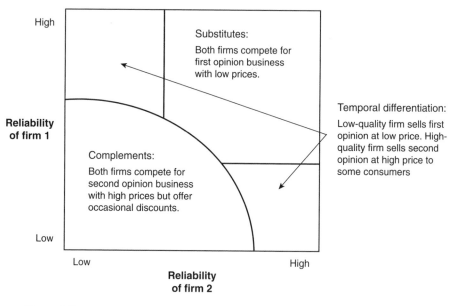

Figure 3.2
Market outcomes on the perceptual map with two independent information vendors

"surprised" by the content of the first opinion) will consult it. On the upside, however, a second opinion seller can charge higher prices because its customers are typically more "desperate" to find out the truth.

It turns out that we can again use the perceptual map of information products to find out what happens in these markets.[11] Figure 3.2 presents such a map. It is similar to figure 2.1 with the marked difference that now we do not assume symmetric firms. Instead, we assume that the two firms' products are relatively independent. This assumption is not too restrictive: if the products were dependent (correlated) then this case would correspond to the uninteresting "substitutes" scenario, which is already captured in the upper-right corner of the figure.

Clearly, if information products are reliable or correlated there is little scope for a second opinion market. The second opinion is likely to say the same thing as the first one and as such, has little or no value. In this case, each information seller tries to sell a first opinion to the customer and they will harshly compete on price to do so. In other words, they compete as substitutes and, as a result, firms have no other choice but to set low prices. In this case, there is no qualitative difference between a dynamic market and one where customers buy information simultaneously. Accounting firms selling audit services often face this situation. Since there is little ambiguity about the rules and methods used, there is also little chance that the second opinion will reveal something new. They set a low price to get the client's business. This practice is called "low balling" in the profession.

What happens in private information markets when both information sellers have low reliability and they are independent (the case corresponding to the lower-left corner of figure 3.2)? Although this case is, again, not too different from the case when the purchase decision is simultaneous, the firms' behavior is somewhat puzzling. Clearly, the two competing products will end up being complements: one product alone provides little value but the two together are quite valuable. When information is purchased sequentially however, there is an additional issue: one of the firms has to sell information first. This firm is at a disadvantage though. It takes up the role of screening the market for the other firm, which then benefits by being able to charge a high price to consumers desperate for a second opinion. While the first firm sells to all potential customers (has a large volume), its unreliable product cannot command a high enough price to compensate it for the loss of the very profitable second opinion market. With similar firms there is a problem: both want to sell second. But then, who will sell first? If no one does there is no market for selling second opinions either. One can show that this situation leads to an interesting competitive pricing pattern. Each firm sets the price high to position itself as a second opinion seller. They take turns however, giving random discounts to their customers to maintain the market. To the industry observer, it is hard to identify such situations that tend to look just like the case when consumers buy information simultaneously. In fact, *qualitatively*, private and public information markets behave the same way in this situation. When reliability is low and products are relatively independent they are complements, competition between information sellers is mild, and prices (on average) tend to be high. Sequential sales of information as opposed to simultaneous sales therefore do not make much of a difference.

Imagine now that one firm's reliability is "fine" but the other firm has higher quality information. This case is captured at the upper-left and lower-right corners of figure 3.2. Here, there is an opportunity for what can be called differentiation "*in time*" and this situation is different from the simultaneous information purchasing case. The lower-quality firm, on the one hand, can position itself as a first opinion seller by setting a fair price for its medium-quality product. Its role is either to reassure consumers in their priors or to detect trouble. It is willing to do so because its quality is clearly lower than that of its competitor; in other words, in no way would it ever be hired to provide a second opinion. The high-quality firm, on the other hand, can set a high price and, in this way, position itself as a second opinion seller. Its role is to attend to the needs of decision makers in trouble. Remember Best Doctors in Boston? The firm almost always gets involved when some serious disease has been diagnosed and, consequently, expensive treatment is being recommended by the first opinion. For first opinion seekers, the price is too high to consult this firm first. But for those consumers who are desperate for a reliable second opinion, this firm is the solution.

I call this setup "temporal differentiation," because firms essentially decide to differentiate in the order in which they sell to their clients. The interesting thing about this particular form of differentiation is that the second opinion seller benefits from the existence of a first opinion seller. If it were the only seller of information it would make less profit. The reason is quite interesting. The first opinion seller screens the market for the second opinion seller by identifying consumers whose willingness to pay is really high (remember these consumers are desperate to resolve the uncertainty resulting from the contradiction between their prior and the first opinion). As a result, the second opinion seller can target this segment accurately and raise its price for these consumers. In fact, its price is higher than what it would be if it were the only one selling information. Thus, first and second opinion sellers do not really compete. Quite the opposite! The first opinion seller may even have an incentive to refer its clients to the second opinion seller. In turn, the second opinion seller may honor this service by actually paying for the reference. Such referrals are often the rule in second opinion markets. In medicine, generalists may refer patients to specialists. A lawyer may refer complex cases to specialized legal firms.

How is temporal differentiation implemented in practice? Obviously, there are no physical markets (stores) for first and second opinions. It is the products' positioning that makes temporal differentiation concrete. How do you position your product as a first or a second opinion? Simply labeling information as "first opinion" or "second opinion" is not going to work. Or would it? I came across a legal consulting firm, for instance, that calls itself "The Devil's Advocates." The firm is a pure information seller. It does not get explicitly involved in litigation. Instead, it only provides second opinion in complex cases. As a general rule, the efficient way for information sellers to implement temporal differentiation is, again, through the management of consumer perceptions about their products' attributes: reliability, independence and, of course, price. In other words, information sellers need to make themselves appealing for shoppers of first opinions or shoppers of second opinions, depending on which market they can or are willing to target.

Differentiation in Content, Source, or Time

Now that we have introduced a variety of pricing strategies, it is a good time to pause and discuss the well-known concept of differentiation. Differentiation is an important strategy concept in all product markets. It is one of the fundamental ways to reduce competition and, to the extent that all strategy setting seeks to reduce competition for the firm, differentiation is often the first thing to consider. In information markets, differentiation is a slightly more complicated concept; it may mean a number of different things. While we have touched on many aspects of differentiation, collecting them here nicely illustrates the subtle differences in the information product category.

First, there is of course the traditional meaning of differentiation: the firm seeks to sell content that is different from what its competitors sell. The customers are usually different as well. This obviously leads to reduced competition between information sellers. If I sell information on the future sales of laptops, then I do not compete with another firm selling forecasts on beer consumption. In other words, as with other product markets, such differentiation will lead to some monopoly power in the market segment seeking the specific content in question. Monopoly power in turn translates to higher prices and profits. In this respect, information markets are not different from other product markets.

The second meaning of differentiation—this one specific to information markets—is related to the concept of *independence*. In this context, competing firms sell the same content (i.e., information about the same thing to the same clients) but they use different sources or different methodologies to produce the information. This allows the buyer to combine the two products and arrive at a better assessment of the truth. In other words, it makes competing information products complements rather than substitutes. We have seen that the result in terms of pricing is similar: prices increase and firms make more profits. The important difference compared to the previous case is that now "competing" firms sell to the *same* customers; that is, they do not have monopoly power over different segments. In fact, under complementarity, prices may be higher than monopoly prices.

Finally, we have seen that in private information markets, consumers may buy information sequentially rather than buying all information at the same time. In these markets, the real strategic issue is that consumers' need for information may change over time. After looking at the first piece of information, their need for further information may change dramatically. As a result, firms need to decide whether they want to sell first or second opinions. That is, firms need to differentiate themselves from their competitors in terms of "time." This type of differentiation, again, results in higher prices for both firms. However, the mechanism that leads to higher prices is different from the preceding two cases. Here, what makes the sale of a second opinion really profitable is the screening of the first opinion seller. Those who seek a second opinion have a high willingness to pay for it.

Ignorance Is Bliss: The Case of Information Cascades

So far we have looked at static and dynamic information markets and have seen the subtle differences between them. In both cases however, the key driver of information pricing was the reliability and independence of information products. These essential features of information prescribe when is it beneficial *to combine* different sources of information, which in turn determines competitive dynamics. But the sequential acquisition of information may hold special traps for information buyers and sellers. These traps can be so severe that they might stop people from using information at all.

As an example, imagine the familiar situation where you have to choose between two restaurants.[12] The two restaurants (say A and B) are next to each other and they have just opened for business. Both have received similar reviews in the media with a slight—really insignificant—advantage given to restaurant A. People arrive at the restaurants in sequence at dinner time and they observe the decision of the previous person by watching him or her enter one of the restaurants. In addition having read the reviews in the media, each person has also received some private information, say a rumor, about which restaurant is better. These rumors—like most rumors—have some error, of course, but their reliability is the same for all people. Moreover, the rumors are independent from each other.

Now imagine the following scenario. One night there are 100 people coming to have dinner and everyone except the first person has received a rumor that restaurant B is better. The first person is the only one who has received a rumor that A is the preferred choice. In this scenario, it is obvious that restaurant B is almost surely better than restaurant A. Although there is some evidence to support A—namely the meager prior information provided by the media and a piece of rumor received by one of the potential customers—the vast majority (99 percent) of the *independent* information available supports restaurant B. No matter how unreliable the rumors are, since they are independent, there is a very high chance that restaurant B is truly better.[13]

But how will people behave in their choices? The first person arriving to the restaurant—let's assume she is a woman—will choose A without hesitation. After all, she has her rumor as well as the slight hint of the media supporting restaurant A. The second person—say, a man—has a dilemma though. He has his private rumor saying B but he has observed the previous person choosing A, which tells him that her private rumor must have been A, otherwise she would have never chosen A. So the second guest knows two pieces of rumor now: his own (indicating B) and that of the woman entering restaurant A before him (indicating A). As these two signals have the same reliability they cancel each other out and the remaining information—that provided by the media—breaks the tie. As it slightly favors restaurant A, the best choice of the second guest is to choose A as well. Thus, the second guest ended up in restaurant A *regardless of the private rumor that he personally received.* As a result, his information is of no use to the next guest because it does not get revealed in his behavior. Now, let us consider the third guest, say, another man. He sees someone enter restaurant A right in front of his eyes. But he does not learn that person's rumor from this behavior because that person's decision was independent of his own rumor. As a result, the third person's problem is exactly the same as that of the second person. He only knows that someone before must have had a rumor saying A and he has no clue about the rumors that other people held. He ends up ignoring his own signal and follows the person with the A rumor blindly. The same logic applies to the fourth guest and so on until everyone ends up in restaurant A, despite the overwhelming available information clearly indicating that this is the wrong choice.

This is a classic example of what is called an information cascade. It is one potential mechanism behind the collective behavior that people call "herding." The basic idea behind herding is that despite plenty of information supporting a particular option, people choose another (usually suboptimal) option because they somehow find it useful to mimic each other. The common notion of herding suggests that somehow people are "stupid" to follow the crowd. What is interesting about this example, however, is that the outcome is based on the assumption that everyone is perfectly rational. Each person carefully calculates all possible outcomes using all the information available. Unfortunately, the situation is such that a small unlikely event results in everyone making a mistake. Here, the fact that the first person's rumor supported restaurant A made everyone else ignore their own signals. If for whatever reason the second person had followed his own signal and ignored the first person's behavior, everything would have been fine.

Follow the Herd

There are many examples of information cascades in the real world. It is hard to verify if herding originates in an information cascade or some other mechanism, but there is plenty of anecdotal evidence—some quite well documented—that suggests that information cascades do exist. In his book *The Wisdom of Crowds*, James Surowiecki describes a couple of well-documented cases, some with a negative outcome and some with positive outcomes.[14] Plank-road fever in the mid-nineteenth century in the United States is one example of an information cascade that misled investors for decades, creating a huge bubble. Daniel B. Klein and John Majewski have thoroughly documented how in a general public "mood" for improving infrastructure, the early success of a few plank roads (wooden planks laid over two lines of timber) in some regions of rural America triggered an investment frenzy giving birth to thousands of plank-road companies throughout the United States.[15] It took decades for investors to realize that the roads did not last and after about four years required heavy maintenance. What is remarkable is that none of the thousands of companies that entered the industry verified the viability of the plank-road business. The industry had to produce massive failures before the concept was thoroughly scrutinized. Once its major weaknesses were exposed the idea was completely abandoned in the second half of the 1800s.

Not all information cascades are bad, however. Some information cascades can result in unambiguously positive outcomes for society. In one of his other examples, Surowiecki describes how William Sellers, a smart entrepreneur, managed to steer the fragmented screw industry toward adopting a standard for screws—his own design, of course. In many ways, the emergence of particular standards can be seen as information cascades. While they do not necessarily result in the adoption of the ideal design (a classic example being the QWERTY keyboard invented in 1876), the mere fact that people "herd" to adopt a particular standard is beneficial for society.

Modern times of course have their own herding behaviors. Recent examples include the Internet bubble of the 1990s, the subprime investment frenzy in the mid-2000s, or, at a smaller scale but with equally painful consequences, investors' support for Bernard Madoff's $50 billion Ponzi scheme for decades before it got exposed in the middle of the 2007 credit crisis.[16] In all these cases, the early success stories of a few people make late comers ignore their own information about the decision. As more people fall into the trap, the stronger the case becomes for following them. With the benefit of hindsight, we know, for instance, that Madoff could not present compelling evidence to investors about the superiority of his investment strategy. In fact, he could barely show evidence that he had a legitimate business going on. It is unlikely that investors would have accepted such meager data and put their money in any other fund. They did it in the Madoff case because they ignored the direct information in favor of the indirect information implied by other—sometimes famous and sophisticated—people's behavior. And again, the more such people behave wrongly, the less there is an incentive to look into one's own information. As Madoff's case shows, information cascades can persist for quite some time.

Selling Information in a Cascade

How is an information cascade relevant for information sellers? At first sight, it seems that such a market is great for information sellers. With all the rumors floating around, it might make sense to go out and purchase some information rather than just blindly follow the crowd. Unfortunately, this is not really the case. Remember that in our restaurant example people deliberately decided to ignore their private information. In other words, the value of private information is low because people anticipate not using it. Only if the potential new source provides much more reliable data than the so-called rumors might a decision maker decide to pay for it and use it. The challenge is, of course, that information cascades tend to be born in highly uncertain environments, where generating good information is difficult. In the case of a private investment fund, such as Madoff's, the whole point is to buy into a proprietary (and, therefore, secret) trading strategy so the fund will legitimately guard the secret of this trading strategy for itself. Similarly, we have seen that in the 1990s Internet bubble, forecasting technology trends was difficult and many respectable firms (Forrester and other research firms covering technology) could only provide very unreliable information. So, if history provides a strong prior supporting a particular decision, it becomes harder and harder to convince oneself to purchase information.

Another problem is that people observing each other's behaviors have an incentive to free ride on each other's thirst for information. By construction, information cascades emerge under circumstances when one's behavior is *supposed to* reveal one's private information. We have seen that in this case, no one has an incentive to buy information. Of course, in the case of information cascades, the whole problem originates from the fact that people's private information is not getting revealed in their behaviors because people prefer to ignore their own information. Nevertheless, when it comes to paying for extra information the free-riding problem remains. Why should I be the one investing in the education of the whole market? Why should I be the whistle blower?[17]

The bottom line: in information cascades the demand for information is low. Combined with the fact that good information is hard to produce, the information market is likely to be weak, which further contributes to the ignorance of decision makers. The key takeaway is that dynamic information markets, while potentially very profitable for both low- and high-quality information sellers, can also represent a danger for the markets' very existence.

Monopolists, Cartels, Collusion, and Regulation

Clearly, competition in information markets is unique. Depending on the information products' characteristics as well as on the timing of decision makers' purchases, a variety of unusual market outcomes may emerge. How should regulators deal with this peculiar product category to ensure fair competition and efficient markets? What can regulation do to avoid market failures caused by information cascades? To answer these questions, let's explore what is it like to be a monopolist in an information market.

The answer is quite simple and, at first sight, does not differ that much from what we find in other product categories. When information is of high quality, being a monopolist is great! But being a monopolist in an information market where products have low reliability is not that much fun. In the latter case, a single product has little value to consumers so the monopolist cannot ask for a high price. So far, there is little difference between information and other products.

But how does the low-quality monopolist fare compared to the case when it faces competition? If the monopolist faces a competitor with an independent perspective then suddenly consumers may be more interested in its products. By cross-checking the two "competing" products, consumers can get valuable information for their decisions. One can show that—as is usual for complements—a monopolist may be better off inviting a competitor in the market than staying alone.[18] In fact, as we will see in chapter 7, there are situations when a single firm is better off introducing its own competitor.

What about cooperation between firms? It is usually illegal but at the minimum it is controversial. While subtle cooperation between competing firms is a reality in many industries, open collusion between competitors is forbidden by antitrust authorities and constitutes a criminal offense leading to serious punishment for the firm and its executives. In light of the law the issue is: what is open collusion and what is subtle and sometimes "legitimate" cooperation between firms? We will not be able to settle this debate here. Multiple courts relying on high-profile experts often fail to do so. Rather, we will consider a clear case: the issue of open price fixing by firms.

Open price fixing is unambiguously illegal. But should this rule apply to information products? The principle behind forbidding price fixing is that it leads to a cartel, which therefore increases prices, which eventually hurts consumers. There is an important underlying assumption however. It is that competing products are substitutes. Because most competitive markets satisfy this assumption we tend to assume that it is always the case. As we have seen, in information markets competing products are not always substitutes. They are only substitutes when the information is reliable or sources are not independent, or both—in other words, when information products cover areas with limited uncertainty. In these cases the rule applies: collusion or price fixing by firms leads to increased prices and this hurts consumers.

When the information supply is ambiguous and highly uncertain, and when methods to produce information are not well established and suppliers have different perspectives, information products are complements rather than substitutes. Price fixing by firms has a different effect in this case. Instead of increasing prices, it leads to a decrease in prices. This is surprising, but the explanation is quite simple. It has to do with the fact that for complements, firms tend to overprice. A firm's problem is not to win the customer's business over competitors but rather to secure the largest possible slice of the pie that the customer is willing to spend on the bundle of information products. If firms can coordinate their prices they are less aggressive in their quest to squeeze the maximum out of consumers' budgets for information and the total price of the bundle decreases. Of course, consumers are better off with lower prices. Moreover, firms are also better off: with a lower total price for the information bundle, more consumers can afford it and the market becomes larger. The increase in the size of the market largely compensates firms for decreased prices. In sum, when information products are complements, collusion makes all market participants better off, both consumers and firms. If regulators understand this then collusion should be allowed in certain information markets. Turning the argument around, firms should be able to convince regulators that their information market consists of complements.

As we have mentioned, regulators have a strong role in making sure that information markets can exist in the first place. Copyright laws, for example, are essential in this respect. It is also clear that some public intervention may be needed to ensure the existence of information markets when market failures are likely, for example, when people rely heavily on each other's behavior to obtain guidance for their own decisions. This aspect of regulation is quite intuitive. What defies intuition and our natural reflexes is how to regulate competition between information sellers. As we have seen, under some conditions allowing price fixing may help not only firms but consumers as well.

Key Lessons

1. Prices and profits in information markets with unreliable (and uncorrelated) information are likely to be high—higher than monopoly prices and profits. In contrast, when competing information products are reliable, they are substitutes and firms engage in harsh price competition leading to low prices and seller profits.
2. Competing information sellers therefore may find it beneficial to advertise the *unreliability* of their products to make buyers perceive them as complements.
3. Complementarity and substitution also play an important role in markets where consumers buy information sequentially. However, in such markets a viable strategy for a somewhat higher-quality seller is to specialize in selling second opinions only. Differentiation may then designate three separate strategies in information markets: differentiation (1) in

terms of content, (2) in terms of correlatedness or independence, and (3) in terms of "time" as first and second opinions.

4. Dynamic information markets may represent a danger for information sellers because they may lead to information cascades, where decision makers refuse to use their own information and blindly follow each other's decisions. In such cascades, the demand for information is usually very low.

5. Regulating information markets is tricky, because with unreliable information products, a monopolist seller may be better off with a competitor and collusion (a cartel) between information sellers may lead to lower prices benefiting buyers as well as sellers.

4

Why Information Sellers May Lie

We have been assuming that information providers are honest. When we considered "low-quality" information our assumption was that the information provider does her best to provide the right information, but is susceptible to making mistakes. On average, however, she is right and if we had access to enough independent providers we would eventually get close to the truth. In the language of statistics, we assumed that the information providers were "unbiased."

When buying information or evaluating its quality, knowing whether the information is biased or not is of crucial importance to the decision maker. But what is *bias*? Common usage suggests that biased information tends to "lean in one direction" or, more generally (in the context of decision making), it tends to favor one decision over another. Defined broadly in this way, is bias always a bad thing? Not necessarily.

Bias as Wisdom

To understand bias, we need to revisit our discussion of priors in chapter 3. Remember that for every decision there is always some prior information, which can be considered the sum of beliefs that allow one to make the decision right now, without gathering further information. A prior could relate to some evidence or to the reliability of some *type* of evidence (e.g., from a certain measurement technique).

Understanding the nature and origin of priors is important in assessing whether favoring one decision over another is good or bad. For example, an information seller may have a special perspective on the decision. This may mean that he systematically distrusts certain evidence (pays little attention to it) but gives significantly more weight to other data. One could say then that the information coming from this seller is biased. However, the buyer of information may value this bias. Imagine that the information seller in question is a doctor looking at various lab results. Based on his knowledge of how the human body works and the technologies used in the lab, he decides what weight should be given to which results and symptoms to determine the disease, which in turn defines the appropriate treatment. In fact, the added value of his diagnosis is precisely the proper interpretation (weighing) of the raw data. Bias in this sense is generally a good thing and would be synonymous with "expertise."

Some people might object by saying that expertise is objective while bias is subjective and uncontrolled. Well, not quite! Think about the number of people who decide to change doctors because they do not trust their expertise (perspective). In more extreme cases, some people distrust the mainstream medical perspective altogether and follow alternative medicine (e.g., homeopathy). In other words, when it comes to making decisions in uncertain situations expertise is almost impossible to measure objectively. The bottom line is that taking one's prior into account should not be considered a bias with a negative connotation. It simply reflects the information provider's inherent beliefs, which may be of great value to the decision maker.

If one doesn't understand the nature of priors then casual observation of real-life data can easily lead to false conclusions about an information market. Consider figure 4.1, for example. The figure shows annual real GNP growth rates (represented by the connected triangles) and their forecasts (represented by circles) from the *Business Week Investment Outlook* survey for the period 1972–1993. Respondents belonged to a panel of economists who were asked to predict a number of economic indicators for the subsequent year. It is striking to see that forecasters tend to make the same mistake: the circles tend to be on one side of the triangle in each year. One can quickly jump to the conclusion that forecasters are "herding." Even though there is considerable discrepancy in their statements, for whatever reason they all tend to either overestimate or underestimate the truth.

This phenomenon does not necessarily mean that forecasters are herding, however. As I argued earlier, an honest forecaster reports his true belief about future GNP growth, which is the weighted average of his prior and the private data that he has obtained through his research. What is the prior? It is the mean GNP growth that he expects *without* his private information. Chances are, however, that his fellow forecasters have the same prior (after all, the mean growth of GNP has been observed to be the same by everyone). Then when the truth turns out to

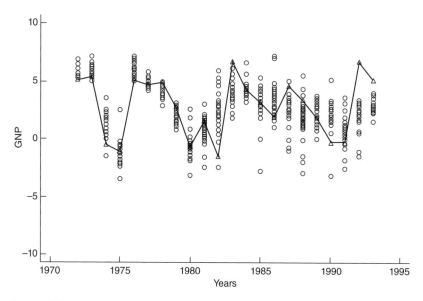

Figure 4.1
Annual real GNP growth rates (triangles) and experts' forecasts (circles) *Source*: *Business Week Investment Outlook* survey for the period 1972–1993 as reported in Lamont 2002. Copyright Elsevier 2002

be above the prior mean, the honest forecasts all tend to be lower than the truth because each forecaster has pulled back on his private information toward the common prior. The opposite is the case when the truth is below the prior mean. The more the truth deviates from the prior mean, the more it is likely that the forecasters miss it in the direction of the mean. In fact, in figure 4.1 we can see this tendency: 1974 (just after the "oil shock"), 1982, and 1991 are all years where GNP changes a lot compared to the previous year. In all these occasions, each forecast is way over or way under the true value of GNP. In summary, even without herding, the existence of a common prior will make the forecasts look similar to one another. But again, this similarity is okay. Do we want our information providers not to take into account the common expected "wisdom" about the truth? Of course not!

The bottom line is that taking one's subjective beliefs into account should not be considered to lead to biased information. What is bias then? Bias is when information sellers lie. Instead of reporting their real belief about the truth they report one that they don't honestly believe. When would they do so and why? Let's explore such situations next.

Partisan Bias

Information providers may of course lie when they have an interest in the decisions that their diagnosis or forecasts help to make.[1] This is the so-called partisan bias. It may often emerge when the information seller has other business activities that are actually linked to its information sales business. When I take my car to the mechanic, for instance, I usually get a terrible diagnosis with major repairs recommended immediately. This is partly because I have an old car. But still, the diagnosis cannot be entirely true and I always ignore part of it. I am always thinking: is the mechanic going to be honest, knowing that there is a high probability that he will be asked to fix the diagnosed problems? Probably not! There is no doubt that it is in his interest to overstate the seriousness of the problem and then benefit from the higher revenue linked to the business of fixing it. Many information markets face this issue. One is medical diagnosis, which may imply an expensive treatment. Although most doctors are well intentioned they may have an incentive to overdiagnose the problem if they also deliver the treatment. In their book *Dance with Chance*, Makridakis, Hogarth and Gaba show plenty of evidence that doctors' diagnoses are usually biased in the direction that implies expensive and often unnecessary treatments.[2]

Another example is management consulting when the consultant is also a major supplier. In the late 1980s, for instance, IBM started an ambitious management consulting business. Analysts were very skeptical about the service's future. They argued that IBM would have a great problem convincing its customers that it provides independent advice. Strategic decisions in modern organizations often have important implications for the client's IT infrastructure. IBM, a major IT equipment supplier, could have a hard time claiming an unbiased position on its clients' strategic situation. IBM managed to prove analysts wrong and its consulting operation has turned out to be quite successful. It is now responsible for more than half of the firm's profits and in 2002 IBM even bought PriceWaterhouseCoopers' consulting arm to become one of the largest management consulting firms in the world. At the beginning, however, IBM needed to establish its reputation for independence. One measure it took was to allow its consultants to recommend equipment from other IT manufacturers.

The Case of Credit Rating Agencies

Interestingly, while partisan bias is a well-known problem it persists even in areas where eliminating it would be relatively easy, with corresponding benefits that are far from negligible. One example that attracted a lot of attention in the 2008 credit crisis was the business of credit rating agencies (CRAs). Many have denounced CRAs as one possible source of the credit crisis. The business press took up the subject in great detail.[3] And this is not the first time. After the burst of the Internet bubble in 2001, CRAs got similar attention for the following two years.[4]

CRAs are typical information sellers. As their name indicates, credit rating agencies evaluate financial assets (including institutions and countries) in terms of their credit worthiness. The primary goal is to make comparisons possible. In Standard & Poor's terminology, for instance, an AAA rating means a "top investment" while D means "default." BBB- and BB+ are intermediate ratings. Such ratings are regularly used in investment decisions and in all kinds of other financial transactions. In fact, ratings are deeply embedded in financial regulation. For example, money market funds are largely limited to holding only highly-rated short-term assets. Or, the Securities and Exchange Commission (SEC) uses CRA ratings to determine how much capital a broker-dealer needs to maintain on its books. Similarly, regulators often require mutual funds, for instance to use CRAs to value their assets or justify their investments. A good rating may mean access to valuable credit but, by the same token, the consequences of getting a bad rating from one of the agencies can be devastating. For example, in 2008, when the CRAs suddenly soured on mortgage-backed securities and other collateralized-debt obligations (CDOs), suddenly all financial institutions looked severely undercapitalized, putting the entire financial system at risk of failure. The basic idea behind credit rating agencies is, of course, investor protection. This is arguably a noble cause and maybe this is why the role of CRAs has constantly increased in financial regulation up until the credit crisis. So what went wrong?

First, like many other information sellers, rating agencies sell highly unreliable information. Assessing the risk of complex CDOs is complicated and depends on many assumptions about the state of the economy in the future. Recent history is full of evidence showing that CRAs are often wildly wrong in their ratings. Besides misreading the risk in mortgage-backed securities and other "structured" products, CRAs' most frequently cited "errors" also include overlooking warning signs of the collapse of the Internet bubble, failing to predict the 1997 East Asian crisis, and not foreseeing the bankruptcies of Enron and WorldCom. In 2010, CRAs were criticized again for not foreseeing the European sovereign debt crisis.

A second issue is that relying heavily on CRAs may distort the market because their ratings may become self-fulfilling prophecies. As more and more institutions (including regulators and banks) assess credit risk based on the agencies' credit ratings, a rating downgrade can easily trigger higher-interest payments for the borrower, putting it in more financial difficulty and, as a consequence, leading to an even worse rating. In the extreme case, this vicious cycle can even lead to bankruptcy for the borrower. A similar vicious cycle led to massive bank failures after 2008 when the agencies changed their minds on CDO ratings and banks' capital suddenly proved to be insufficient.

But putting aside the criticisms with respect to the agencies' "mysterious" methodologies and the inherent risk in so strongly relying on them, the most important problem is what specialists call "conflict of interest." CRAs make their profits from the fees charged to companies whose securities they rate. Furthermore, they often sell advisory services to these clients. Clearly, they have a strong incentive to keep their clients' ratings higher in return for business. In other words, CRAs represent the typical example of partisan bias.

When confronted with such criticisms, CRAs counter by saying that nothing matters more to them than their reputation, a concern that prevents them from being biased. But until the mid-2000s this claim was difficult to believe in light of the fact that their business was protected by regulation. Indeed, the second problem with CRAs was that until 2002 there were only three of them: two larger ones, Moody's and Standard & Poor's and a smaller one, Fitch. This limited oligopoly was primarily secured by regulators, namely the SEC, which is the only authority with the power to issue the status of "nationally recognized statistical rating organization" (NRSRO). For almost thirty years, the three agencies enjoyed their protected market and took over any newcomer that achieved NRSRO status. After 2002, following the crash of the Internet economy, the SEC started to become serious about imposing competition among CRAs. By 2005, two new agencies managed to impose themselves: Dominion Bond rating service in 2003 and A. M. Best in 2005.[5] Although there were about ten CRAs "competing" with each other by 2009, the financial regulatory system remained somewhat schizophrenic about ratings agencies. For example, in 2009 the Fed's lending programs accepted only collateral that was rated by a "major" rating agency, which meant of course one of the big three.[6] This, of course put at a serious disadvantage the smaller, new CRAs trying to establish themselves on the market.

This ambivalent attitude toward the regulation of CRAs is very surprising, especially since research in economics has established that competition is a good remedy to the problem of partisan bias.[7] Clearly, with only a few agencies closely watching each other's ratings it is difficult to believe that strong rivalry exists among them. While the SEC has stepped up efforts to increase competition in the CRA industry (in particular, reforms were introduced in 2006), the 2008 credit crisis showed that these efforts were largely insufficient. The Dodd-Frank Wall Street Reform and Consumer Protection Act (the Dodd-Frank Act), signed into U.S. law in July 2010, goes much further in regulating CRAs. Not only is competition ensured, but also the SEC is controlling CRAs much more tightly. It now oversees their methodologies and business models and requires reports to monitor the possibility of conflict of interest. Europe is considering similar laws. From January 2011, the European Securities and Markets Authority (ESMA) will directly supervise ratings agencies. The European Commission is considering rules similar to those introduced in the United States targeting the transparency of the agencies' business and competition.[8]

Partisan Bias and Reputation

Partisan bias in the domain of financial markets is far from being unique to credit rating agencies. After the burst of the Internet bubble, the industry that has generated the most controversy with regard to partisan bias is investment banking. Since the stock market crash at the end of the 1990s, the business press has provided extensive discussion about the conflict of interest between investment banks' investment activities and their financial analyst business.[9] "Famous" analysts, with quasi-star status at the end of the 1990s, like Mary Meeker or Henry Blodget, were now criticized for being partly responsible for the Internet bubble by providing extremely favorable valuations for the so-called dot.com stocks even after their valuations started to collapse. The criticism was one clearly related to partisan bias. Investment bankers who are bringing an initial public offering (IPO) want optimistic forecasts in order to place shares at high prices. Similarly, stockbrokers have an incentive to provide positive forecasts for shares to attract new buyers and earn additional trading commissions as fewer clients want to short. As such, analysts working for these institutions have huge incentives to provide biased information.

Anecdotal evidence seems to support the claim that analysts are under pressure to bias their forecasts upward to generate more business for their institution's brokerage arm. Stories circulate in the financial press about analysts who had to leave their brokerage house for not following the optimistic forecast often generated by the management of companies. One of these examples mentioned in a study by Hong and Kubik concerns

Henry Blodget himself, who was hired to replace Jonathan Cohen at Merrill Lynch—one of the world's largest brokerage houses—because the latter stuck to traditional valuation methods that did not go along with management's optimistic forecasts.[10]

Similarly to credit rating agencies, brokerage houses counter with the argument that the accuracy of analysts' predictions is what builds analysts' reputation, and this is more important for their carrier concerns than the aforementioned pressures. In contrast to the case of CRAs, however, this argument seems credible because analysts face fierce competition. Their accuracy is regularly measured and published in various outlets. For example, the magazine *Institutional Investor* regularly polls money managers about analysts' performance on various criteria closely linked to forecast accuracy (e.g., perceived expertise in earnings forecasts or stock picking). Analysts' ranking in the poll is highly visible and known to be important for their carrier.

Given these opposing arguments, it is important to ask what motivates analysts more: partisan bias or reputation concerns? In recent years, many financial economists have analyzed data to answer this question and the evidence seems to clearly side in favor of partisan bias. For example, Michaely and Womack show that stocks that underwriter analysts recommend perform more poorly than "buy" recommendations by unaffiliated brokers.[11] In their careful study, they also explored alternative explanations to partisan bias. One such explanation could be based in psychology—namely, that analysts are framed by the fact that their firm is an underwriter of the IPO. This effect is similar to parents' evaluation of their children as "special." In other words, the bias is inherent in the analysis and constitutes the analyst's true belief. In contrast, independent analysts are more open minded in their evaluations and thus end up making better forecasts. Another explanation is that underwriting firms have been chosen by clients precisely because they have a favorable view of the client company. In other words, an analyst's overly optimistic evaluation is due to a selection bias. Again, this explanation excludes the idea that the analyst changes his recommendation *intentionally* because of personal interest. Michaely and Womack ran a small survey with investment professionals asking which explanations they favored of the three: partisan bias, framing, or selection bias? The overwhelming majority of their respondents favored the partisan bias explanation. More interestingly, 100 percent of the investment professionals on the buying side favored the partisan bias explanation, while only 73 percent of the investment bankers—still an overwhelming majority—sided with it.

The study by Hong and Kubik provides even stronger evidence for the partisan bias of investment banks' analysts.[12] They studied a large panel of information on the brokerage house employment and earnings forecast histories of about 12,000 analysts working for about 600 brokerage houses between 1983 and 2000. While they did not have data on the analysts' earnings, Hong and Kubik tracked their career moves across brokerage houses, which have a well-defined hierarchy of prestige. In this way, they could indirectly measure which analysts did better than others and relate their career advancement to their forecast history. First, they found that forecast accuracy is indeed rewarded. Inaccurate forecasters have a high chance to move down the brokerage house hierarchy. But accuracy has to do with variability, not bias. In terms of bias, the data shows that—controlling for accuracy—analysts who issue more optimistic forecasts (relative to the consensus forecast) are more likely to experience a career move up. Moreover, analysts were found to be judged less on accuracy when it comes to stocks underwritten by their houses. Furthermore, in this case, their (lack of) optimism was significantly more important in explaining downward carrier moves. Finally, Hong and Kubik also found that this was truer during the last four years of the Internet bubble than for the period before. These findings provide strong evidence that partisan bias plays an important role in stock analysts' forecasts, which in turn begs the question: why didn't regulators separate these seemingly incompatible activities to better protect investors? The Dodd–Frank Act, mentioned earlier and aimed at the regulation of the financial sector seems to wake up to the challenge.

Over the years, information markets have evolved in a direction where information products tend to become decoupled from related goods and services that may bias the information traded on these markets. This is partly due to the development of technology. Technology made many information markets a legitimate business by allowing such decoupling to occur. Part of this trend however, is also due to competition. Independent information vendors that are perceived to be unbiased by customers have an advantage over their competitors who cannot claim such independence. But partisan bias remains strong in many information markets.

Bias from Independent Forecasters

The preceding discussion suggests that, as long as we keep the information business separate and independent and we ensure fair competition among forecasters, information markets will provide unbiased information. In turn, even if this information is inaccurate combining multiple sources may result in quite accurate forecasts.

Unfortunately, this is not true. Competing information providers may have an incentive to lie even if they have no interest in the decisions that will be made based on their forecasts. Among others, macroeconomic forecasters typically fall into this category. They only provide advice and are exposed to quite extensive public scrutiny in various media. At the same time, macroeconomic forecasting is a competitive business. Those who are successful in predicting key economic indicators are not only rewarded by markets but also by governments. Alan Greenspan, for example, practiced economic forecasting before being appointed to the Board of Governors of the Federal Reserve and, subsequently, as its chairman.

It turns out that it is competition itself that may push even independent information sellers to be biased. Anecdotal evidence actually supports this view. We have already mentioned herding by risk-averse forecasters. Herding is widely believed to be the practice of risk-averse forecasters trying to defend their reputations. However, there are many other practices. In his study, Lamont surveys the popular press to reveal lesser known strategies that may help information sellers beat the competition.[13] "Scattering," for example, is one such technique whereby the forecaster tries to stand out by providing unreasonable forecasts (either in a positive or negative direction). The main motivation, of course, is to draw the market's attention onto her. Another practice is called "broken-clock" strategy and it consists of always forecasting the same event. Lamont mentions a famous example, that of A. Gary Shilling, a well-known "recession-caller" during the 1980s, who systematically provided the lowest forecasts about the economy. The problem with this anecdotal evidence is that it is contradictory. Are forecasters herding or do they have an incentive to stand out? If we can observe different behaviors, under what conditions should we see one versus the other?

In recent years, academic research has systematically explored these questions. Among others, a remarkable study conducted by Ottaviani and Sorensen reveals fascinating dynamics among competing forecasters.[14] Their research shows that forecasters' bias and its direction depend on the actual way they compete and the way they are rewarded. They highlight two qualitatively different types of competition among forecasters: (1) contests and (2) reputation building. Then they show that depending on the nature of competition, forecasters will tend to bias their forecasts in different directions.

Contests among Forecasters

Forecasters often compete in a contest-like situation. How do contests work? The information providers are evaluated on how close they get to the truth—that is revealed later—and the winner(s) get a reward. Such contests are often explicit in the world of forecasting and their rules are announced in advance. For example, macroeconomic forecasters are ranked by their relative accuracy in the semiannual Wall Street Journal Forecasting Survey. *The Wall Street Journal* runs similar competitions for earnings forecasters and "stock pickers" (these are the WSJ All Star Analysts and WSJ Best on the Street, respectively). A number of rankings are available on Internet sites. For instance, Validea.com and BigTipper.com rank Wall Street professionals based on the performance of their stock recommendations. Contests exist for noneconomic variables as well, for example, the National Collegiate Weather Forecasting Contest.

One would expect that such contests—all based on "accuracy"—will push forecasters to become as accurate as possible. Not quite. An important aspect of contests is that it is not sufficient to be good, but one has to be better than the others. Rewards are disproportionately higher for the top ranks and may not even exist or may even be replaced with penalties for the lower ranks. This creates weird incentives for competitors. Ottaviani and Sorensen show that the information providers have an incentive in contests to overstate their predictions by neglecting the common wisdom or prior.[15] This strategy resonates to the "scattering strategy" mentioned by Lamont.

But why would forecasters do so? As we have seen, a forecast is produced from the appropriate combination of the private data that the forecaster has and his or her prior information. Clearly, there is an incentive to report the right combination in order to be on the mark. The problem is that competitors think the same way. As a result, many forecasts will tend to be in the region of the truth. The chance to do well among all these competitors is low. Thus, there is an incentive to move away from the "crowd" and differentiate from the other forecasters. The best way to do this is by putting more weight on the private data available to the forecaster (hence less weight on the prior). By doing so the forecast will become less accurate (hence have a lower chance to be on the mark) but it will be more unique (with a higher chance to be the *only* such forecast). In a contest, the forecaster is willing to give up some accuracy to move away from competing forecasts. The independent observer will see more forecast variance as all information vendors will provide bolder forecasts in their quest to "stand out" with their unique perspective.

It is important to see that the fundamental reason for this strange behavior is the existence of a common prior. As we discussed with regard to figure 4.1, this prior pulls forecasts together, in this way increasing competition between forecasters. If there were no prior then the forecasts would be honest. In this case, forecasters would have no indication of how to move away from their competitors' forecasts so they would just reveal their true beliefs. A stronger prior (one that should be given more weight) makes this effect even stronger by making forecasters even bolder in a contest. In other words, the more trust there is in the "common wisdom" shared by the information market, the more forecasters have an incentive to become "bold" with their predictions in a contest.

Forecasters Competing for Reputation

Information providers may not always compete in a contest, however. Often, they compete for the reputation for being well informed, that is, having access to good and unique data. In other words, here they don't really want to be better than the others. Rather, the market evaluates them on how well informed they are, meaning, on how accurate their *private* data is. Ottaviani and Sorensen show that in this case information providers will also lie but in the other direction: they will underweight their private information and, as a result, will become overly conservative.[16]

Why is this? The best forecast of the truth is again an appropriate combination of the data and the prior. More talented forecasters—who can generate good data—will likely obtain private data close to this truth. Thus, it pays to pretend to have such data. Since the truth lies somewhere between the private data and the prior, the forecaster needs to pretend to have received data consistent with the truth, that is, data closer to the prior. Said differently, the further away the forecaster's private signal is from the prior, the higher the risk that it is away from the good forecasts. As a result, there is an incentive to underweight his own data and thus "shade" his forecast. This is what is traditionally called herding. Interestingly, as in the case of contests, it is the existence of a common prior that causes forecasters to herd.

Obviously, the mechanism described only works if the information sellers do not have much information about their own and their colleagues' inherent capabilities. In other words, we have assumed that this capability is solely inferred from the forecasts that they provide. Clearly, if one of the forecasters knows that she is better than the average then she would have less incentive to shade her forecast than a forecaster who knows that he is worse than the average. In fact, the good forecaster should try to weight her private information more to stand out from the crowd. So if forecasters know their own abilities, exaggeration may be an alternative strategy to herding even if they care about their reputation. Another complication is that forecasters understand that the buyers of information may figure out their incentives—as is the case in reality—and they may adjust their behavior accordingly.

Empirical evidence supports that information about forecasters' abilities mediate the effects of competition. In his paper, Lamont finds for instance that older forecasters, with presumably more experience and more confidence in their ability, tend to deviate more from the consensus forecast (or the common prior).[17] In another paper, Chevalier and Ellison find that older mutual fund managers have bolder investment decisions, which again is consistent with the preceding arguments.[18] This pattern is also backed by another empirical finding, namely that less experienced equity analysts seem to herd more than their more experienced colleagues.[19]

The bottom line is that nonpartisan forecasters will tend to herd if they worry about their reputation, are not sure about their ability, or actually know that their ability is low. If forecasters are facing competition in a contest, or know that they are above average in their forecasting ability, then they have an incentive to exaggerate. Ottaviani and Sorensen argue that all these effects end up actually decreasing the accuracy of forecasts.[20] They conclude: "The analysts' desire to be perceived as good forecasters turns them into poor forecasters." Maybe this is why economic forecasters have such a bad reputation altogether. In its June 3, 1995 issue, *The Economist* magazine reported the results of an unusual survey.[21] Ten years earlier, in December 1984, the editors asked four ex-finance ministers in developed economies, four chairmen of multinational firms, four students at Oxford University and four London garbage collectors to predict a variety of economic variables (growth, inflation, and exchange rate) for the next ten years. In 1995, *The Economist* compared the forecasts with the facts of what actually happened. The article publishing the results shows that the dustmen's predictions fared as well as those of the so-called experts.

The implication for buyers of information is that they need to figure out how their potential information sellers compete to try to correct for these biases, or at least be aware of their existence.

Media Bias and Biased Consumers

If one speaks about bias in the context of information markets, one cannot avoid mentioning the controversial topic of media bias. Consider the following example. In September 2004, during the U.S. presidential campaign, the Texans for Truth group began airing television ads questioning whether President Bush had fulfilled his military obligations in the National Guard decades earlier. On Tuesday, September 14, 2004, *Fox News* published the following report about the event:

President Bush's National Guard record is now under assault by a group calling itself Texans for Truth. The group is a branch of DriveDemocracy, an Austin-based organization that has received seed money from the liberal-leaning anti-Bush group, MoveOn.org. ....The group this week is releasing an ad in which a former lieutenant in the Alabama Air National Guard says neither he nor his friends saw Bush when he supposedly was with their unit in 1972. The president served as a pilot with the Texas Air National Guard and sought a transfer in 1972 to work on a political campaign.

On the same day, *CNN*'s report said:

The founder of the group Texans for Truth said Tuesday that he is offering $50,000 to anyone who can prove President Bush fulfilled his service requirements, including required duties and drills, in the Alabama Air National Guard in 1972. ....
The Texans for Truth group began airing television ads questioning whether Bush fulfilled his military obligations. Its name is a takeoff on Swift Boat Veterans for Truth, which has been airing ads questioning the military record of Democratic nominee Sen. John Kerry. That group's allegations are at odds with the official Navy records and Kerry's former crew mates.

Similar examples abound and cover a variety of topics. Two Harvard economists (Gentzkow and Shapiro) introduce their study on media bias by reporting three versions of a firefight between the U.S. military and Iraqi insurgents, each provided by a different media outlet (*Fox News, New York Times,* and *AlJazeera*).[22] Their example is similar to the one preceding: while each media report is factually correct, each provides strikingly different impressions for the reader by selectively omitting certain details or emphasizing some facts more than others. This is what is commonly called "slanting," which results in media bias.

The existence of media bias is commonplace. It is recognized by the average person in the street as well as academics and political leaders. Examples are widespread and span all events affecting our lives, from sports to war. They also concern both past and current actions of well-known personalities, with special attention given to politicians. Some of these biases and their impact have been documented in great detail, as in DellaVigna and Kaplan's paper "The Fox News Effect: Media Bias and Voting." [23] Beyond such academic examples, media bias is a topic in a variety of popular discussions and publications. In the November 18, 2001, issue of the *New York Times Magazine,* Ajami covers at length the differences between Arab and American media in covering the Middle East.[24] A variety of books document media bias in U.S. national media. After the 2001 presidential election, at least four books appeared about media bias in favor of both Left- and Right-leaning political parties.[25]

What is the reason for media bias? More important, in a free world where media can compete openly, how can media bias survive? While our previous discussions of bias indicate that it can subsist even under competition, here, the situation is clearly different because the bias is readily *visible*. Some media are so openly biased that even their regular readers recognize it. For example, according to the 2010 biennial media consumption survey of the Pew Research Center for the People & the Press, 82 percent of Americans say they see at least *some* bias in the news and 52 percent say they see *a lot*.[26] Perceptions of media bias depend, of course, on political views: Democrats generally see more conservative bias (36 percent) than liberal bias (28 percent), while Republicans generally see liberal bias (69 percent). What is also interesting is that regular audiences see more bias in the news than the public as a whole, so people seem to actually experience media bias. People remain generally skeptical about news organizations. In 2010, no more than a third of the people surveyed by the Pew Research Center claimed to believe *all or most* of the reporting by fourteen major news organizations.

The public's view on the source of media bias is quite straightforward. Most people believe that the media are somewhat controlled by strong interest groups that have a direct interest in influencing public opinion. This view—which is very similar to the argument of partisan bias—is not far from the truth in many situations. In nondemocratic countries, for example, governments clearly manipulate the media to hide information from the public. The control of media by politicians is a more controversial subject in free democracies. In Italy, for instance, there is a heated public debate about Prime Minister Silvio Berlusconi's extensive control over the national media, a large chunk of which he owns. Berlusconi owns three analog television channels, various digital television channels, as well as some of the larger-circulation national news magazines.[27] The debate over Berlusconi even spread to the international scene when *The Economist* published an article openly criticizing him as an "unfit" leader for Italy.[28]

Similar debates have been raised concerning Rupert Murdoch, the media mogul who controls large fractions of the media in many countries through his company, News Corporation (News Corp).[29] Although Murdoch is not a politician, he considers himself a libertarian. As a result, his newspapers have been accused of conservative leanings in comparison with other national newspapers. For example, people claim that during the buildup to the 2003 U.S. invasion of Iraq, all 175 Murdoch-owned newspapers worldwide editorialized in favor of the war. News Corp-owned Fox News is often criticized for its alleged Republican or conservative bias, or both. Whether these allegations are true or false is independent from the fact that a strong political agenda supported by a large media owner combined with the lack of strong competition has the *potential* to lead to strong media bias. In this sense, the public's view of media bias is right. The problem is that media bias is ubiquitous and typically exists even when competition is strong between media outlets. In fact, recent research shows that competition may cause it.

Media Bias and Differentiation

How can competition cause media bias? In their pioneering study, Mullainathan and Shleifer argued that media bias exists because the consumers of media content are themselves biased and—more important—they seek information (news) that is consistent with their biases.[30] As would be the case in any product market, media firms tailor their news messages to the needs of their consumers, delivering biased views. What we observe under competition, then, is nothing else than media firms differentiating themselves from each other, each competing firm taking a position away from the others, catering to a given consumer segment. From the perspective of an outsider, each media firm appears to slant the same news to please its target audience.

This view of media bias is consistent with other research on how people consume the news provided by the media.[31] On the consumer side, psychologists have documented that people indeed prefer information that is consistent with their existing beliefs. They find it more credible and remember it better than information that is at odds with their priors. It was also found that people actively seek out information that is consistent with their beliefs. This evidence is in striking contrast with our earlier discussion of priors, including the idea that people supposedly weight their original beliefs and add that result to the new information they receive, in order to generate an *updated* view of the world. Instead, it seems that people consume news to reassure themselves and confirm their priors.

This view of media is also consistent with the perspective of media firms. The practice of "slanting" is referred to in communications literature from the 1940s.[32] Furthermore, it is well accepted in media circles that news cannot be delivered to the public in the form of data and facts but needs to be embellished in coherent stories that deliver a certain point of view, a practice commonly referred to in media circles as the so-called narrative imperative.[33]

While this theory of media bias as applied to news seems to hang together and is quite plausible, there is one problem: news described this way—in other words, as information slanted to please an audience with certain preferences—does not classify it as an information product. Remember, we have defined information products as information that is used for decision making. Here, news is clearly used as a source of pleasure or psychological reassurance, more like entertainment rather than the source of information for deliberate decision making.

But is this the case for *everyone*? While it is clear that many people consume news as entertainment, some people clearly watch the news to discover facts and act accordingly.[34] For these people, news is nothing but an information product. The real question is: how will media bias affect these people? In other words, the market for news is a dual market. On the one hand, a large segment of people consume news for entertainment. On the other hand, a relevant consumer base consumes news as an information product. How will this latter segment be affected by the existence of the first one?

Interestingly, media bias might actually not hurt those who seek information. In their study, Mullainathan and Shleifer calculate the welfare of a *hypothetical* "conscientious reader," in other words, a person who only cares about the truth but has to gather information from the biased media.[35] They find that the conscientious reader is better off with competing biased media than with a single unbiased medium. The explanation is somewhat familiar: competition makes the media more biased because media firms try to position themselves away from each other. By doing so, they have a captive audience to which they can charge high prices (or sell their "eyeballs" to advertisers). However, in their effort to be biased the news outlets need to generate extra information on top of what is readily available. If they were to report only the facts, then they wouldn't be able to convey their point of view. Instead, they need to discard (downplay) some of the existing information and find new evidence (additional experts, different pictures, more background, etc.) to report. If a conscientious consumer cross-checks the different media firms' news messages, she will end up having more accurate information than if she were to listen to a single unbiased medium that doesn't have the incentive to find and offer extra information. In other words, under media competition, news may be biased but the total amount of information available may be higher.[36] So media bias is not necessarily bad.

One question remains, however. What if these conscientious readers are active rather than hypothetical market participants? In real life, there are people who read news for information—hopefully. Would the media be less and less biased as the number of conscientious consumers increases? A colleague Yi Xiang, and I have examined what would happen to a market where media firms compete for two types of consumers (1) biased ones, as in Mullainathan and Shleifer's study,[37] who are only interested in hearing news that is consistent with their beliefs; and (2) conscientious ones who are only interested in learning the truth.[38] We thought that if we assumed that conscientious readers are active participants of the news market, then media firms would adapt to their demand and reduce their bias. Surprisingly, we found the opposite: competing media firms became even more biased as the number of conscientious readers increased. Why?

The answer is intriguing. Media firms realize that if conscientious readers are conscientious enough then they will look at multiple news stories and cross-check them to learn the truth. We found empirical support for this. In the 2004 survey by the Pew Research Center 25.6 percent of the consumers claimed to regularly listen to both *Fox News and* a major Democratic news channel. Just like our consumers in chapter 3 who considered two unreliable information products as complementary, conscientious readers/viewers are ready to pay for two news items to discover the truth. On the one hand, however, by doing so these consumers become a captive audience and price differences across media will not affect their behavior. On the other hand, the biased consumers always choose the medium that is closest to their beliefs as long as prices are not too different. In fact, the more the media are biased in the opposite direction—that is, the more the news is differentiated—the higher the prices because there is less competition for biased consumers. With the presence of conscientious readers media firms have an incentive to increase prices to earn as much as possible from this captive segment. How to increase prices? By taking an even more extreme position. In this way, differentiation from the competing media firm is higher and prices can rise.

This seems quite depressing. Conscientious readers have little hope (other than the prospect of government regulation): they need to pay a high price for the truth. Fortunately, the situation is not all that bad. We found that even with higher prices and increased media bias, the conscientious consumers may be better off than without media competition (only having a single, albeit unbiased news outlet). But the outcome is not unambiguous. It depends on the relative proportion of conscientious readers compared to biased consumers. On the one hand, if conscientious readers represent either the majority or the minority of news consumers, they "benefit from" media bias. On the other hand, if conscientious readers represent an intermediate proportion, they are worse off with media competition. The exact cutoffs depend on the media in question, as well as the distribution of the different priors of biased consumers. The main takeaway is that news markets are not just information markets, and their dual audience has a very strong influence on their competitive landscape as well as on their efficiency in reporting the truth.

Key Lessons

1. Bias may be wisdom if it reflects the information seller's prior information.
2. Decision makers combine different information sources as well as their own prior beliefs when they form *updated* beliefs about events. In the presence of a broadly shared common wisdom, correlated forecasts may not be evidence of herding behavior from information sellers.
3. Partisan bias may contaminate an information product if the information seller has a direct interest concerning the event to which the information refers. Competition usually helps reduce partisan bias.
4. However, even nonpartisan information sellers may bias their information if they compete with one another. If they compete in a contest they will try to stand out by exaggerating their private information. If they compete to improve their reputation they may herd by shading their forecast.
5. Media bias in the context of news may result from large proportions of listeners who listen/watch/read news for entertainment and enjoy news that is consistent with their priors. Media competition leads to more media bias because of differentiation.
6. In a competitive media market, the presence of conscientious readers who only care about the truth may not eliminate media bias. It might actually increase it. However, the total amount of information generated in a competitive media market is higher than under a monopolistic medium.

II

Bringing Information to Market

In part I, we studied the economics of information. Based on well-established decision theory, we developed the demand for information products and explored how information sellers compete when faced with this demand. We looked at the information industry from the top as a regulator would do. We saw that compared to other industries, information is a peculiar product, for which its sellers tend to follow quite unusual strategies for pricing and for differentiating themselves from their competitors.

In part II, I would like to change the reader's perspective. Rather than looking at the collection of competing information sellers, we will look at the specific things that a specific information seller needs to do in order to develop, package and distribute, advertise, promote, and research the information or knowledge that is meant for sale. In other words, this part of the book deals with how the information business should be organized to be successful.

Chapter 5 starts by exploring the *value chain* to see how different players in the information business (from data vendors to analysts and consultants) interact in adding value to help clients make decisions. It is crucial for an information business to decide where to enter the value chain and how to integrate with upstream and downstream partners.

Next, we will look at the *value delivery system* of an information seller. Chapters 6, 7, and 8 address the four key elements of the value delivery system. In chapter 6, we study the different *channels* through which information may be distributed. These channels have undergone enormous change in recent years and have created much turbulence in the industry. Chapter 7 looks at *information branding*, or how to efficiently communicate and promote information products. Finally, in chapter 8, we will look at the *R&D function* of information sellers. How can one generate new information and knowledge? What tools and infrastructure are available? More important, how did new technologies change the R&D landscape for information and knowledge sellers?

5

The Information Value Chain

Data, Information, and Knowledge

The word "information" has many synonyms including "data" or "knowledge." How do these relate to each other and to the idea of a single product category, product market, or industry? Data may be used to help decision making as do knowledge and information, and all of these may be purchased and paid for. So far, we have considered all of these as "information products." For a firm, however, it is important to decide in which of these businesses it intends to compete.

Data and knowledge are extremes on a continuum, which measures how much value the product adds to the specific decision at hand. From a business's perspective the data-knowledge continuum is in fact the information industry's *value chain* (see figure 5.1).

At the "low" end of the value chain is *data*, which—at the extreme—can be any sequence of code (numbers, letters, etc.). At the minimum the data should also specify the context it refers to. *Information* is more than data. In addition to context it also refers to patterns and regularities that are present in the data. Take, for example, a sequence of numbers representing a set of temperature measurements in a particular geographic location for a given time period. We can safely call this data. Analyses of the data could reveal cycles with repeated patterns over time. These patterns can be referred to as the relevant information in the data. *Knowledge* is still more than that. Beyond context and patterns it also contains causal links between the patterns present in the data or even between multiple different data sets. In the temperature example just given, for instance, finding an explanation to the patterns among geography, time of the year, and temperature using other resources (e.g., laws of physics or other data on the motion of planets, or both) is what really makes the information valuable for decision making. It is the patterns together with causal links

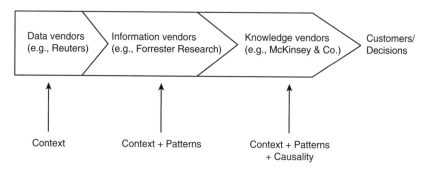

Figure 5.1
The information value chain

that lead to understanding, which ultimately makes decision making really powerful.

Clearly, the boundaries between data, information, and knowledge are quite blurred but the basic idea is: the more context and causal structure are added to data, the higher the information product is in the value chain, or the closer it is to the decision itself. At the extreme, one could imagine a firm, which sells the service of actually making the decision for the client. Strategic management consultants are in this business, and come close to providing this service because their advice often reflects the solution to a concrete business problem. Obviously, the decision maker who "buys" this service believes that the advice is based on knowledge, itself created through the analysis of data and information. In sum, one can think of the consulting service as a knowledge product: the knowledge or insight that forms the basis of the decision.

Information sellers can be categorized along the information value chain. In table 0.1, for example, data vendors include Thomson Reuters and Bloomberg, to name only two well-known companies in the domain of finance. These firms' core activity is to produce and sell financial data to their customers. Information sellers add considerably more structure and analysis to the data. Take financial analysts, for example. Financial analysts would use the data provided by these data vendors and identify patterns and trends in various sectors. Similar information sellers exist for other industries as well. Forrester Research, Gartner, Jupiter, Meta, and the Yankee groups, for instance, are all well-known analysts for the high-tech industry. They publish industry trends and forecasts in various product markets from information technology to mobile telecommunications and Internet commerce. Information Resources Inc. (IRI) is a market research firm in the fast-moving consumer goods sector. Its core product is the analysis of Universal Product Code (UPC) data generated by supermarkets' point of sales. Some analysts are narrower in their focus. EMCI, for instance, is a small boutique specialized in selling analyses and forecasts only for the mobile telecommunications industry. Finally, many professional services firms can claim to be in the knowledge business by creating and delivering "knowledge" or the actual decision (solution) for their customers/clients. In the financial sector, investment banks would typically cover this activity. Strategic Management Consultants like McKinsey & Co., The Boston Consulting Group, Bain & Co., and many others provide high-level, knowledge-based advice for virtually all industries. Advertising agencies, accounting firms, as well as law firms can also be thought of as typical knowledge businesses.

The Taxonomy of Information Products

Using the value chain and the notion of "private" and "public" information markets mentioned earlier, one can build a useful "map" of the various sectors of the information industry. Figure 5.2 draws this map by considering (1) firms' position in the value chain (i.e., on the data–information–knowledge continuum), and (2) whether they sell public information (i.e., face the demand from mass markets) or whether they sell private information (typically facing the demand from niche markets). Figure 5.2 positions on the map some of the examples that we have seen so far.

Glancing at the map, one can quickly see that, in practice, it is hard to find firms that are at the lower-left or higher-right extremes of the map. In particular, there is no real market for "private data." Rather, firms selling such data usually also add more value to it and end up selling information or knowledge. Similarly, it is hard to find vendors of "public knowledge." In other words, the two dimensions of the product space represented on the figure are not completely independent. Firms that sell private information usually have products that are closer to knowledge. This is not surprising. If the information is produced for a broad customer base it is hard to make it equally relevant to everyone. Financial information, for instance, is used in a variety of ways by Bloomberg's customers. Some use it for investment decisions, while others use it for accounting and valuation purposes. In contrast, if information is collected for a specific customer, it is easier to put it in the context of that particular customer's decision problem and add more analysis and structure to it.

	Data	Information	Knowledge
Public (Mass market)	**Data vendors** (Google, D&B, ThomsonReuters, Bloomberg) **Credit rating** (Moody, Standard & Poor, Firch)	**Market/Industry research** (Forrester, Gartner, IRI, AC Nielsen)	
Private (Niche market)	**Accounting services** (PWC, E&Y, KPMG) **Medical lab results** (Hospitals)	**IT consulting** (Accenture, IBM) **Strategy consulting** (McKinsey, BCG, Bain) **Medical diagnosis** (Best Doctors)	

Figure 5.2
Taxonomy of information products

The Information "Value Net"

So far, we have considered the information industry's structure in isolation. But as is the case for all industries, the value chain of an industry is not isolated in the economy. Therefore, to complete the picture, it is useful to draw the industry's so-called value net that represents the connections of the value chain to other industries' value chains. Figure 5.3 draws a simple representation of the information industry's value net. One way to think about the value net is that it is the infrastructure or the platform of the industry. Without this infrastructure the industry would have a hard time existing. The value net is to the information industry what operating systems are to application software. It is to the industry what roads are to the transportation industry. Also, it is through these connections (this interface) that the information industry affects all other parts of the economy.

On figure 5.3 I divided (quite arbitrarily) this infrastructure into public and private sectors. Private infrastructure can be thought of as the collection of organizations that are "complementors" to the information industry. In essence, they are responsible for creating other products and

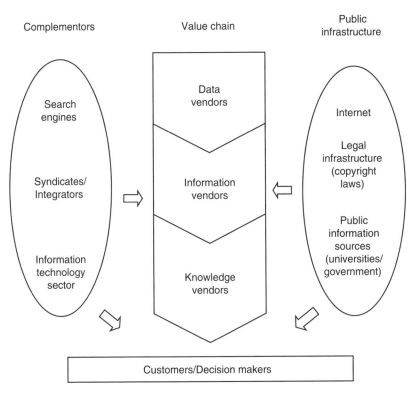

Figure 5.3
The information value net

services that increase the value of information products. Think of information technology, for example. Information has always been stored and transported somehow: first engraved on a stone plate, later written on paper, then printed, and today, usually stored on some digital medium (e.g., a computer hard drive or a CD). Each of these technologies made it more convenient to store information, thus adding value to the core product category. In this way, the development of these complementary industries has contributed significantly to the growth and change of the information industry. Similarly, the public infrastructure is instrumental to the industry's progress. Here, special attention should be given to the legal infrastructure that provides the ground rules for all players: consumers and competitors as well as complementors. Some of the most exciting questions related to the future of the industry arise while these ground rules are being created. For example, as the Internet has become a key part of the global public infrastructure for information products, the community of nations is wondering about its regulation (or the lack of it). Any decision on this front will have a major impact on the industry's evolution. Similarly, the rules that will govern competition among credit rating agencies will have a huge effect on the functioning of the entire financial sector. In sum, considering the value net, that is, the extended value chain is important because some of the most interesting questions arise from analyzing the information industry's interface with other parts of the economy.

Now that we have drawn the rough boundaries of the information industry, we can ask the question: where in its value chain should the firm compete? The rest of this chapter is devoted to this question.

Selling Data versus Selling Knowledge

Should a firm sell data, information, or knowledge? Clearly, knowledge is more valuable for decision making so it represents higher revenue potential. However, it is generally much harder to create. Usually, this translates into higher costs. Furthermore, the market for a knowledge product is likely to be smaller. A data set can be sold to a large customer base (as it may be relevant to many decisions) at the tiny cost of copying it on another hard drive or CD. In contrast, a consulting assignment is not cheap to reproduce and is likely to be irrelevant for even similar decisions of other customers. This trade-off—revenue potential versus production costs (so-called scalability)—is an obvious consideration.

For example, Dun & Bradstreet is a well-known information company providing company credit reports, risk evaluation reports, and sales and marketing solutions. One of the key value propositions of D&B is "objectivity." Objectivity is clearly a positive benefit for customers but it also constrains D&B to a data market. The company actually made a conscious decision not to move into the domain of "advice" where judgment is involved and objectivity is threatened. Advice, while highly profitable, is left to other information sellers. The reason underlying this decision has to do with D&B's culture and core competences. The company is good at two things: (1) research, in other words, gathering hard data from a variety of sources, and (2) information technology, especially database and network technologies. While the first ensures the appropriate coverage of the market, the second makes sure that databases are reliable, and the information is available when and where needed. Timeliness and accuracy are key virtues of the company. Clearly, competing in the knowledge business would require a very different expertise. Instead of generating and organizing data, much more emphasis would need to be given to analysis, interpretation, and background industry knowledge. In light of D&B's existing core competences, staying in the data business seems to be a reasonable strategy.

But—as in any other industry—there is another issue to consider and that is competition. Where will a firm likely face higher competition, in the data market or the knowledge market? In the data market, of course! First, traditional ways to avoid competition—such as differentiation—are easier to implement in knowledge markets. Data is data while a complex set of arguments based on various analyses may look very different even if it is based on the *same* data. As knowledge products typically contain a fair amount of subjectivity and judgment (think about the alternative diagnosis provided by a doctor based on the same lab results), competing products will likely represent multiple perspectives. More important, judgment almost certainly implies "low reliability" compared to data considered to be "hard" information. As we saw in chapter 3, these factors are likely to lead to very different competitive forces depending on the firm's position in the value chain. In data markets, there is a higher chance for providers to compete as substitutes. In contrast, in knowledge markets complementarity between providers is more likely. In turn, complementarity leads to less competition and higher prices.

In sum, knowledge markets require core competencies and production technologies that are harder to acquire, manage, and sustain, but knowledge markets tend to be less competitive. There is more scope for differentiation, personalization of service, and most important, for complementarity between sellers. A decision maker is more likely to buy two industry reports on his industry than buy two data sets to analyze the industry. The recommendation then seems to be obvious: data vendors facing increased competition should gradually move to knowledge markets. But in practice, this is not so easy. Although data vendors had all the incentives to make the transition, given the increased competition in the data sector due to the emergence of the Internet, success stories for repositioning a firm as a knowledge vendor are rare.

D&B is no exception. At the end of the 1990s, with the rapid development of information technologies and the Internet, data vendors' core competences were becoming less and less sufficient to secure competitive advantage. By the end of the decade, the Internet had become a pretty reliable and cost-efficient distribution system for information, so one didn't necessarily need IT experts to obtain and analyze data. Suddenly, the barriers to entry in the information business collapsed because there was no more need to build the large IT infrastructure for data storage and distribution.[1] What competitive advantage remained to large data vendors such as D&B? The answer: the extensiveness of their data coverage. This, indeed, was hard for a newcomer to match. However, it is far from clear how the "completeness" of the traditional data vendors' databases could be leveraged for competitive advantage. Newcomers argued: who needs a complete solution when different suppliers of information on the Internet can be conveniently repackaged and provide the information buyer with a customized interface at relatively low cost?

For D&B the question was: would it make sense to move higher up in the value chain at the cost of completely changing the profile of the firm? Under the new strategy, the firm would sell "knowledge," in other words, consulting services. Database managers and network specialists would need to be replaced with statisticians and economists. Would D&B's unique, extensive data coverage provide competitive advantage under this new business model? Chances are that the answer is "yes"! When only the data is sold, coverage only means convenience. Convenience is an important benefit but it is threatened by competing proprietary and public (Internet) networks providing comparable convenience. However, when knowledge is generated from the data, extensive coverage is key to ensure the *quality* of the advice provided. D&B has an opportunity to turn its huge databases into high-quality insights through analysis. However, this would mean painfully changing the company's profile. To be fair, the company does emphasize the marriage of "information and analytics" on its website. Still, in the public's mind D&B is clearly a reliable data provider rather than a "trusted advisor."

Reuters' Struggle from Data to Knowledge

D&B is not the only data vendor to struggle with these issues. Reuters, another famous player of the financial information industry, has been facing the very same problems. In 2000, just when the Internet bubble burst, Reuters seemed to have a quite bold and unambiguous approach to the problem of increased competition. Faithful to its century-old reputation for accepting and endorsing radical shifts in technology, it made a major commitment to the emerging Internet medium. At the end of 2000, it decided to transfer all of its services (that were previously based on its proprietary network) to the Internet. The operation was estimated to last for four years and cost $725 million.[2] Was this just a change in distribution technology? It didn't seem so. Reuters realized that the new public network, called the Internet, is much more than a cheaper version of a traditional distribution vehicle. The Internet is an interactive medium that—as we will argue in the next section—can be deployed not just as a distribution channel but also as a powerful technology to *produce* information and knowledge. The idea that a network can be turned into a powerful medium for transactions from just a simple transportation vehicle of information bits was not unfamiliar to Reuters, one of the pioneers in the development of electronic trading systems. As such, in 2000, in parallel with the infrastructure change, Reuters also shifted its services toward providing more content, analysis, and knowledge beyond simply selling data. In June 2000, it colaunched Radianz, an independent global financial communications network based on Internet protocol (IP). The idea was to build a community based on some 60,000 Reuters' customer contacts in over 120 countries. This is exactly what the World Wide Web is about: mass interactivity and community building. Beyond Radianz, Reuters made other efforts to move higher up the information value chain by including significant consulting capabilities to its services lines. The company's revenues originating from consulting or other knowledge services quickly increased to a respectable 7 percent.[3]

However, these enthusiastic early plans didn't really succeed largely due to their timing. At the beginning of the new millennium, Reuters' efforts were challenged by a tough economic environment that hit the financial and IT sectors particularly hard. This was not a good time to propose a major structural shift to investors, who expected quick return to profitability. In its effort to focus its strategy and improve the bottom line, in 2005, Reuters sold Radianz to British Telecom along with a variety of other businesses.

In 2008, Reuters merged with the Thomson Corporation to form Thomson Reuters, to become one of the world's largest financial and general news providers. It remains to be seen if Thomson Reuters can pull off a major shift in strategy to address the threats and opportunities that the revolution of mass interactivity brings to the financial information industry. The company's communications certainly seem to indicate a move in the right direction. Positioned below the company name, the new tagline "Knowledge to Act" supports the general positioning of a knowledge vendor rather than that of a data provider.

Value Proposition for Information Products

Once the firm has decided where in the value chain it wants to compete, the next step is to develop a value proposition for its customers. Although in practice this is usually a quite difficult exercise, conceptually it is simple.

The value proposition is a formal statement that defines the target customers, lists the key benefits offered, and claims the relevant advantages that the product offers compared to competitors and substitutes. As we have seen in chapter 2, to build a viable value proposition, the firm needs to start with the analysis of its customers' decision problem. Once this is understood the value of information can be calculated and the information product can be compared to competitors'. Subsequently, an appropriate price can be set.

Of course, the problem is that in most cases the firm may not know the exact value of its information to its customers. Furthermore, this value is likely to differ across members of the customer base. However, this aspect of the information business is not different from other products and services, where a deep understanding of the customer base is also necessary to develop meaningful value propositions. As a general rule, if the customer base is small and very specific to the product in question then it is easy to figure out the relevant offering and set the right price. This is what would typically happen in a private information market.

In contrast, in public information markets, customers are diverse in their decision problems and, as a result, their needs for information are also very different. Firms use various techniques to address such customer heterogeneity, including product customization or bundling among others. While these techniques can be also found in other product markets, in information markets they can be pushed to the extreme. This is because one aspect of information makes the product category particularly appealing for these techniques, namely information products' cost structure. With a few exceptions, information products typically have high fixed costs and low (sometimes nonexistent) variable costs. The following selling formats all exploit this particular feature of the information product category.[4]

Versioning

In most public information markets it is almost impossible to assess each customer's needs, and so the information vendor has to consider some sort of an average. A single average product with a single price for the whole customer base, however, seems wrong as a strategy. Clearly, the information seller can do better by coming up with a few *versions* of the product for different *customer segments*. Most companies face this issue in selling any product to a large customer base. It is called discrimination. They have to group customers in different sets with similar needs and provide a value proposition to each group. How many groups (segments) should a firm serve with a different version of its product? The answer usually depends on the trade-off between the increased revenues generated by a finer segmentation strategy and the costs associated with the production of multiple versions of the same product.

Here is where the cost structure of information and knowledge products plays an important role in managing this trade-off. In most cases information products have high fixed costs and very low (sometimes practically zero) marginal costs. Think about the production of an industry report by Forrester Research. Generating the first report is a laborious task that involves many hours of research by highly trained specialists. Once the first report has been produced, however, producing an identical report costs only the price of the paper on which the content of the first report will be copied. If reports are distributed electronically, the cost of "producing" subsequent copies is even lower.

The cost of coming up with multiple versions—or *versioning*—is also quite low. If Forrester Research figures out the likely evolution of the market for a particular new disk drive, it is easy to produce a less sophisticated version of the report. The company just needs to delete a few details. Say, it could provide the likely sales figure for the overall market, but state that the client needs to buy another version if he is interested in knowing how the market will fare in distinct geographic regions, or two years down the road, or depending on some other variable. In fact, it is relatively easy to come up with multiple versions of the report where each version is a less elaborate copy of the "master" report. Versions with higher sophistication command of course a higher price and will be purchased by customers who need to know the market details for their decisions. Other customers, who just need a ballpark figure on the overall market size, would be happy to buy a cheaper version that contains less information. By carefully designing the quality of the versions, and setting the appropriate price for each, the information seller can increase the total value extracted from the customer base. A further advantage of versioning is that the firm doesn't necessarily need to know which customer wants what. It only has to figure out the distribution of customer needs. If the versions are well designed, customers will self-select for the right product offering.

Extensive versioning (or *discrimination*, as it is called by economists) works when producing multiple versions is cheap and when customers differ in their willingness to pay for quality. In the context of information products as we have defined them here, versioning is particularly powerful. Decision makers often need various levels of detail and accuracy when they purchase information. In fact, in many public information markets customers often differ in the level of precision they require from the information seller. They wouldn't mind having better information, but they simply do not want to pay for it. In these cases we are talking about *vertically differentiated* markets. In such markets, customers only differ in their willingness to pay for quality but they all agree what quality is (e.g., they all prefer a more detailed report to a less detailed one as long as the price is the same).

Bundling

Not all information markets are differentiated vertically. In *horizontally differentiated* markets, consumers differ in the kind of information they need in the first place. For example, all CIOs are likely to be interested in Forrester's research on the evolution of the disk drive market, although at various levels of precision. CEOs, however, will read *The Wall Street Journal* to find information on a variety of totally different things. The *Journal* is a collection (bundle) of content loosely linked by the broad theme of business. Its audience is very diverse, and the differences across this customer base are not in terms of valuing the accuracy of information but rather in terms of its nature or subject. While few people read all the articles in the *Journal*, each subscriber is likely to find something interesting in it. Creating separate information products for such a market would be extremely difficult. Each article would need to be a separate product, but who would be able to figure out in advance which customers were likely be interested in that particular piece of information? In addition, content changes daily. Pricing such a broad product line with permanent changes would be totally unmanageable. Here again, the cost structure of information products saves the situation. On the one hand, the marginal cost of producing the information is almost zero, so it costs nothing to bundle the products together. The benefit, on the other hand, is huge because consumers' valuation for the bundle is less diverse. Everyone can expect to regularly find relevant and useful information over time. In other words, consumers' valuation for the bundle is roughly the same, or at least significantly less diverse than what it was for the individual items in the bundle. This results in manageable pricing and marketing strategies.

Extensive bundling works when the marginal cost of the items in the bundle is small and the market is horizontally differentiated. Again, information markets fit this category of products particularly well, although bundling may apply to other categories with similar characteristics.

Software is again a good candidate. Microsoft Windows can be seen as a bundle of applications, only a small portion of which is used by any typical customer. Furthermore, bundling in the context of low marginal costs may also help keep competition out if consumers are not sure what exactly they are looking for.[5]

Both versioning and bundling have become much easier and inexpensive to implement with the recent developments in information technology. As electronic distribution becomes more and more the standard for information products, these tactics are used extensively. They may be even combined. Think about the structure of a website. It can be considered a bundle of content, where a broad horizontally differentiated customer base searches for relevant information for a constant subscription fee. Customers looking for the same information may be differentiated further vertically by being offered different levels of quality on the particular topic they are looking at. Higher-quality versions of a particular content area would of course command additional fees for those consumers who are willing to dig deeper in the content.

Information Built to Order

Even though bundling may be convenient for the seller, as it allows him to serve a large and diverse customer base, it may actually be a real nuisance for the buyer of information. Think about an extensive website with all the information available for free at various levels of depth through references and links. Yahoo! is a pretty good example. Once a website has been put together, consumers can surf it to find literally anything. But often this is not what the decision makers want. Instead of wandering around they want precise information about a targeted subject and fast. All other information available makes them less efficient in making their decision. The answer seems to be simple: let us give them what they want. But this leads us back to the old problem of diversity. Consumers are likely to want very different things. What sellers need to do is to make it possible for consumers to customize the broad site for their own purposes. This is exactly what Yahoo! is doing with its MyYahoo! offering. Each member can design the site in such a way that the customized relevant bundle of information appears on the front screen at the time of login. In essence, it is a Dell-type, built-to-order system for information. Internet technology makes this particularly easy to implement. No wonder that other sites from news providers to portals tend to offer similar self-made, tailored interfaces to their otherwise broad content.

Web content may not be the only domain where built-to-order information systems could be easily implemented. Icon Group International (icongrouponline.com), a small Californian publishing company decided to implement it for old-fashioned books.[6] Not just a few books, however: Icon Group offers hundreds of thousands (!) of reference books about products, industries, companies, medical issues, and even countries. For any country, one can get all the relevant information including history, economics, demographics, and so on. The topics of the books are extremely specific. For example, one Icon title is *The 2007–2012 Outlook for Rollerball Pens in Greater China*. Clearly, most of us would not be interested in the topic. But imagine how valuable the book is for the few who do care about it. Where else could they procure a comprehensive source on the market for rollerball pens in China? Consequently, the price of the book is quite high (about $500).

In the domain of healthcare, Icon Group provides reference works for thousands of diseases. One can order, for instance, the Icon book *Aortic Aneurysms—A Medical Dictionary and Bibliography*. Clicking on the title one is sent to Amazon.com, where the picture of the hardcover volume appears with the usual information on prices, customer ratings, ISBN number etc. Below these details is this abstract:

This is a 3-in-1 reference book. It gives a complete medical dictionary covering hundreds of terms and expressions relating to aortic aneurysms. It also gives extensive lists of bibliographic citations. Finally, it provides information to users on how to update their knowledge using various Internet resources. The book is designed for physicians, medical students preparing for Board examinations, medical researchers, and patients who want to become familiar with research dedicated to aortic aneurysms.

Clearly, all these books are targeted to decision makers with a narrow but precise focus. In other words, Icon Group is a hard-core information vendor.

But one might ask: why print books in the first place? Why not make them available on the Internet? This is a good question. Books' days may indeed be numbered. Yet, as a reliable information source, we still like books. Indeed, the format established a strong reputation during the centuries when books constituted the ultimate source for information. Also, books have the advantage that they concentrate and summarize information on a well-defined subject. They are easy to consume and are well organized. They give the perception of completeness on the topic designated by the title. Finally, the book's "low-end" technology ensures that their content is hard to copy for illegal resale—at least compared to a file format or web content.

Besides all these benefits, books have serious drawbacks as well. The main problem with books is that their printing is financially risky. Printing is old technology with huge economies of scale on the production side. A large print run can be done cheaply, but printing a single book is quite expensive. Unless there is enough demand, there is no point in publishing a book. Writing them is not easy either. In the case of Icon Group, how convenient it would be to gather the information on all those medical conditions in one database, rather than write separate text in a book format for each. These drawbacks call the Icon Group model into question—at least from a profitability perspective.

But Icon Group is very profitable, much more profitable than a traditional book publisher. Why? Because it produces its books on demand. No large printing facility is needed. Each book that is printed has a buyer who has already paid for the product a relatively high price. There is no need for physical distribution outlets in the form of bookstores. Consequently, there is no need for the returns policies and discount programs so common in traditional publishing.

Still, one might wonder what happens on the content front. Chances are that *Aortic Aneurysms* only interests an extremely narrow customer base. While it is efficient to print a book for these people, isn't it too expensive to write the book in the first place? Not really. Icon Group automated the writing process itself. It created a patented technology that turns its huge databases about various diseases into books that are enjoyable to read and create the impression that an expert has actually sat down and has typed the whole book from the introduction to the last chapter. In fact, Icon Group doesn't even have its own proprietary database. Its books are based on various databases available for sale on the public data market. Icon Group found a way to integrate these databases and complement them with generic text in the traditional book format that customers enjoy reading.

Icon Group's technology is applicable to any domain for which good data is available, hence the eclectic and wide-ranging medical topics in which Icon Group offers its publications. However, the company's other publications go even further in terms of innovativeness. Icon's country and industry reports are based on various databases as well as Icon's analysis of those databases. Beyond the raw data, these books contain forecasts, correlations, and various statistics derived from the data. In other words, Icon has managed to go beyond offering the book as an attractive format for selling information; it actually generates information in the process.

Moreover, Icon's concept of "automatic content editing" has been patented, and the patent applies not only for the book format but also to any form (interface) in which information can be presented. The company is experimenting, for instance, with generating an automatic news program on TV. Pulling data together from various news providers (essentially journalists), it compiles a "story line" for each news item in generic conversations between two animated characters who act as announcers. While the characters talk, pictures, films, and other data also appear on screen—as is the case for a regular news program. The difference is that Icon's news program has been produced with practically no human intervention. What makes this possible is the availability of a liquid news market, reliable networks that allow transmission of any data in real time, and the application software (e.g., animation technologies) that can repackage information in the required format.

Exclusive Selling

For information products, a key question in terms of the product strategy is whether information should be sold exclusively to one or a few customers or instead be sold to the whole market. This problem typically arises for public information products. In the case of private information, the product is useful only for the customer it has been prepared for, so selling it to others is not possible. In the case of public information goods, where a larger set of potential customers value the product, the situation is quite different. The question here becomes what is the relationship between the potential customers? Maybe there is no relationship at all. A weather forecast, for instance, is useful for a very broad set of people. More important, someone else knowing the weather forecast has no effect on me. I don't really care. Not all information is so neutral though. A market research study grabs the interest of all players in the corresponding industry. Moreover, these players may compete heavily against each other and the information contained in the report may represent considerable advantage in this contest. Whether I am the only one owning the report or others have access to it as well is a very relevant question for the buyer of information. In other words, in this case, the value of information for the buyer is totally different depending on whether he gets the information exclusively or not.

What should the seller do? How should they decide on their exclusivity policy? The question is quite complex and it depends somewhat on the nature and the intensity of interaction between the customers of the information vendor.[7] Overall, it was found that the most relevant question is: what level of advantage does the unilateral ownership of information provide? If this advantage is small then the information seller is better off selling its product to all interested parties. If the information provides considerable advantage for a customer when others do not have access to it, then the policy should be the reverse: exclusive selling is optimal. Customers who receive the information exclusively have a higher willingness to pay for it and this can compensate for the foregone revenues from the remaining market. This basic argument also works when there are multiple competing information sellers. In this case, the general outcome is that they tend to sell to different clients, none of whom wants to be at a disadvantage compared to the others. In sum, the key trade-off that information sellers need to analyze when considering exclusive selling is the size of the potential customer base compared to the increased value of information when it is sold exclusively.

Shared Information Products

In chapter 1, we pointed out that one of the particularities of information products is that they are easy to copy and share with other people. This makes information vendors vulnerable and the enforcement of copyright laws particularly important for the industry. However, no copyright law is perfectly enforceable. What can the information seller do to mitigate the effect of illegal sharing? Furthermore, not all information sharing is illegal. Often, a group may want to share the same information for collective decision making, and it is in the interest of the information seller to meet this demand. For example, management consultants in the same firm may want to share a market research study. One cannot reasonably expect the firm to buy a separate copy of the market research for each consultant. Such a rule would be almost impossible to enforce. In contrast, consider a brokerage house purchasing access to Bloomberg terminals. Here, each broker is supposed to have his or her specific account. Enforcing this rule is very hard though. It is all too easy for brokers to share their account access with their colleagues. The nominal value of similar, illegal information sharing in the financial sector was estimated to be eight billion dollars in 2009.[8]

Interestingly, as long as sharing remains limited, it may not be that bad for information vendors. Specifically, if sharing is limited to small, isolated subgroups of the customer base, and the information seller has some idea of the size of these subgroups, then it can offer a shared information product tailored to subgroups and adjust its price to take into account sharing across customers.[9] Such strategies are not entirely new. For example, a journal subscription is more expensive for a library than for an individual because the seller expects the paper to be shared by multiple readers. Similar strategies exist for other non-information product categories where sharing is easy across consumers (e.g. books, video cassettes and computer games sold to rental stores, etc.). However, in all these traditional examples the seller could readily see the subgroup to be targeted (the library or the rental store). With the emergence of digital storage and distribution of information products, subgroups may form spontaneously and may not be easily observable for the seller. Even in this case, offering shared information products might be beneficial. Interestingly, it is more beneficial, the more there is sharing between the consumers within the subgroup.

How does it work? Imagine that there are three consumers within a group each valuing the information differently. For simplicity, suppose that the three consumers' valuations are $1.1, $1.2, and $1.3, respectively. Let's assume first that copyright laws can be fully enforced. If the information seller tailored its price to individuals and could not discriminate between them then the optimal price is $1.1. In this way, the seller knows that he will be able to sell to all three customers for a total profit of $3.3. Imagine now that the seller knows that the three consumers work together and will share the information product. If copyright is not enforceable, then the optimal individual price is $1.3 for a meager profit resulting from a single sale: $1.3. But what if price were tailored to sharing? The total value that the group gets from the product is the sum of each individual's valuation: $3.6. This is the maximum that the group is willing to pay for the information. The optimal price for the group is therefore $3.6. Notice that the profit made from this pricing scheme is higher than the profit under which a copy was sold to each individual with full enforcement of copyright laws. In other words, pricing shared information products not only can protect the information seller but may actually increase his profits. This is because pricing to the group allowed the seller to tailor price to the sum of the group members' valuations, while individual pricing forced the seller to cater to the lowest individual valuation.

Notice also that if only two people within the group shared the information then adjusting the price to this behavior would make the firm worse off than with full sharing across all three group members. Take, for example, the case when only the first two consumers share the information. Their aggregate valuation is $1.1 + $1.2 = $2.3. The optimal price for the group is $1.3 for the sale of two information products: one for the first two consumers who will share it between them and another for the third consumer. The total profit from this pricing strategy is $2.6, much less than the case when all three consumers shared the information. In other words, if the firm considers the selling of shared information products, it is better off with *more efficient sharing* across consumers within the groups.

Offering shared information products is not always possible. It requires sharing to be limited within subgroups of the customer base but quite efficient sharing among customers within the same subgroup. It also requires quite detailed understanding of the distribution of the size of the different subgroups as well as consumers' valuation for information within the groups. If discrimination across groups is not possible, then the firm needs to choose a careful pricing strategy to maximize revenues. With digital media increasingly dominating the distribution of information products, such strategies will likely be more common over time.

Key Lessons

1. The value chain of the information industry essentially corresponds to the data–information–knowledge continuum. As one moves along the continuum from data to knowledge, more context, structure, and causal relationships are added to the raw data.
2. Firms need to decide where they compete in the information value chain. The choice depends on the trade-off between scalability and profitability. Although information markets are usually less competitive the higher they are on the information value chain (i.e., when firms sell knowledge) they are also less scalable and require more sophisticated R&D and production technologies.
3. Because of their low marginal costs, information products are very attractive targets for well-known discrimination techniques such as versioning, bundling, and built-to-order formats.
4. Exclusive selling of information should be considered when the price charged for exclusivity compensates for the lost volume from the market that is not served.

5. Limited (sometimes illegal) information sharing in the customer base may not always be bad news for information sellers. If information is shared within subgroups of the customer base then information sellers may consider pricing their products to the groups. In this case, the optimal strategy may yield higher revenues than pricing to individuals.

6

Networks, Interfaces, and Search

In chapter 5 we discussed the various product formats that information sellers should explore when developing value propositions for their clients. Once the product is defined, bringing products to market requires another critical task: designing the distribution system. In information markets, this means designing how the information is physically brought to the buyer or user. This aspect of information products is often difficult to separate from other aspects of going to market. In fact, many times it is intimately linked to production as well. A firm's decision to sell knowledge, for instance, almost entirely depends on its production technology and it is literally indistinguishable from its distribution. Consider, for example, a high-level management consulting service. It consists of knowledge produced, sold, and distributed/delivered by the same people, all of whom are an integral part of a consulting team. Or, think of a social network that induces its members to jointly generate shared content, which is then available to everyone. Another example is Wikipedia, the highly successful online encyclopedia. Its users create it. Or think of Google. Is it an information seller or an information distributor? The answer is not clear. Google does not own the information that it presents to its customers. This information is sitting on a website among millions of other sites. But through its algorithms, Google not only presents the requested information but also adds value to it by measuring its relevance. In all these examples, product design, production, and distribution are almost impossible to separate.

Despite this challenge, or maybe precisely because of distribution's central role for this category, we need to discuss the infrastructure on which information travels between sellers and buyers. Specifically, chapter 6 looks at three key issues: (1) the link between information distribution technology and the firm's business model; (2) recent views on networks and search technologies; and (3) interfaces, or the tricky question concerning how information should be presented to its final consumers.

Information Distribution and Technology

More than for any other good or service, the distribution of information products heavily relies on information technology. The reason is very simple. Information products are by definition digitizable. In the last few decades, information technology has provided us with amazing possibilities to store, transfer, and process digital code. Information is a prime category to benefit from this IT revolution. As a result, a large portion of the firms in the information industry could be seen as "distributors of information." Rather than producing original information, their core competence lies in being able to exploit the latest available technology to transfer information between remote locations. In 2002, for example, Reuters launched Reuters Messaging, a reliable, high-security, high-speed instant messaging service developed specifically for the global financial services industry. Reuters, Bloomberg, and many other financial information sellers essentially take information produced at public exchanges and channel it to their clients. Their core value proposition is speed, reliability, and convenience.

However, technological competence for information distributors doesn't simply mean that the latest available technology is used to distribute the same products. Often, a new distribution technology allows the introduction of new products that until then were not available for sale. As we have noted before, the distribution technology may even become the production vehicle for information. Take financial information vendors, for instance. By pulling buy and sell prices together in real time, they are just one step away from facilitating the transactions between buyers and sellers of financial assets. In this case, the information sellers would be responsible for actually *making* the asset market. Asset markets in turn contribute to the creation of price information—in fact, this is one of their key roles. For the information vendor, the strategic question becomes: should I keep generating market data offline and sell it through my network infrastructure or should I connect my customers on a financial market and charge for transactions? Clearly, the two revenue models are entirely different and they are intimately linked to the technology used to distribute information. In fact, the latter choice essentially means that the information vendor moves into a new industry facing new competitors (such as stock or other asset exchanges). This particular example illustrates that each technology breakthrough in the domain of distribution challenges the validity of an information vendor's basic business model.

Few information distributors have been able to successfully navigate the stormy waters of technology development for a long time. Reuters (Thomson Reuters since it merger with the Thomson Corporation in 2008) is one of these exceptions. Through its century-long history, it has constantly been challenged by competitors. Often these competitors exploited a given technology better than Reuters did but few of them managed to survive major technology changes. Even fewer managed to thrive on them. It is interesting to follow Reuters' history and identify the points in time when strategic decisions were made to adapt the business to new technology platforms. Table 6.1 summarizes Reuters' evolution with technology from its birth in the last century through the first decade of the twenty-first century.[1]

The examples that we have discussed so far show that the physical distribution technology for information often plays a key role in actually *defining* information markets. As a consequence, information sellers need to have a deep understanding of the real meaning of technology change. In particular, they need to be able to clearly identify "disruptive technologies" that may produce a qualitative change in the actual content sold.[2] Technological development typically comes in waves. Relatively rare disruptive innovations provide the platform for incremental improvements over longer periods of time. Of course, information distributors need to constantly deploy the newest available technology to remain competitive (either to ensure high-quality delivery of their products or to have lower costs). This is not different from other industries. A key long-term success factor for these firms, however, is to be able to reinvent their business model when a disruptive technology appears.

The Internet and the World Wide Web

In the past two decades we have experienced the emergence and growth of a similar technological breakthrough with major impact on the information industry. This is of course the World Wide Web, which represents the birth of a new mass medium. In one word, the web could be called the medium of "mass interactivity," one that allows "many-to-many" communication. Mass interactivity means a qualitatively new environment for information markets. In this new environment, the difference between buyers and sellers is blurred; information production and consumption have become inseparable; and new technologies have emerged

Table 6.1
Reuters' evolution in light of technology change

Time	Selected key products	Markets	Core new technologies	Competitive advantage	Key competitors
1850	Market news	Investors in Belgium and Germany	**Carrier pigeons** (Horses, Balloon)	Speed (7 hrs.) compared to train	
1851	Market news	Investors in London and Continental exchanges	**Cables, Telegraph**	Coverage outside Europe	Havas Wolff
1860	General news	Newspapers		Expansion in the Far East and the Americas	
1870	Telegrams, Financial remittance (Banking) (Advertising)	Private businesses			
1914					
After WWI	General news	London morning papers	**Radio telegraphy**	Geographic coverage	BBC Havas Wolff
1945–WWII	Commercial news worldwide	Private businesses			Independent telegram companies
1964	Stockmaster (3 digits)	Investors and brokers	**Computers and software**	Speed and market (asset) coverage	US stocknews services
1970	Videomaster (72 digits)				
1973	Monitor ("green screen")	Banks and investors			Association of Swiss Banks
1981	Monitor Dealing Service			Market making	

Table 6.1
(continued)

Time	Selected key products	Markets	Core new technologies	Competitive advantage	Key competitors
1981	Data, analysis and decision support	Financial world	**PCs, Satellite communication**	Availability of information and quality of decision tools	Bloomberg, Telerate, Dow Jones, Citicorp, Swiss Banks, LSE, etc.
1987	Equities 2000			Market making, brokering	
1992	Dealing 2000				
1994	Financial television service				
1996	3000 series				
2002	Reuters Messaging	Financial world	**Internet**	Real-time interactivity, combined with proprietary data and analytics	Financial information vendors, stock markets
2003	Reuters Knowledge				
2006	News bureau in Second Life				

to build, transfer, and manage knowledge within spontaneously formed communities.

The change that mass interactivity has brought to the information industry (and many other industries) is similar to the one electronic trading systems brought to stock exchanges and other commodity markets. It is similar to the impact of broadcasting ("one-to-many" communication as in radio and television) on the advertising industry. As an example, think of search engines that now allow anyone to instantly access information on literally any subject. Think of Facebook and Twitter or other emerging social media in which content can be created, traded, and delivered instantaneously among people located all over the planet. Today, it is increasingly more likely that breaking news stories become available on online social networks before they appear on the official media and even before they are available from professional news providers.

While we still remember the burst of the Internet bubble at the end of the 1990s, we all are witnessing right now the second major wave of investment in interactive technologies and platforms, a phenomenon often referred to as Web 2.0. At the expense of crudely oversimplifying, one could say that Web 1.0 brought two major innovations: e-commerce and search. Web 2.0, in comparison, is really about communities and user-generated content. It is in Web 2.0 technologies that mass interactivity is starting to show its real potential for transforming our environment and, in particular, information markets. What this transformation will bring to information markets is a particularly interesting question to explore.

It might be risky to claim that, at the time of writing this book, one can assess *all* the relevant changes that the web, or more broadly, the concept of mass interactivity will bring to the information industry. I will not attempt to do so. But I would venture to say that, in the context of information *distribution*, there are at least two domains where the web is having a major impact. The first domain is undeniably search. The second is interfaces.

Search and Networks

It is not too far fetched to say that most information can be accessed through the web—if not today, then definitely in the near future. To the extent that information is stored on computers, and the web—by definition—is the set of computers linked to one another across the planet, it is harder to make something not be accessible through the web than have it on the web. Even our personal pictures (not intended for broad distribution) tend to travel attached to emails and sit on servers whose physical locations we ignore completely. The issue is not whether this is safe or whether privacy is in danger—I personally believe that these are not major problems as long as our legal systems function well. The issue is that, *if* one wants to make information available for sale, the web is hardly to be ignored. Even if—ultimately—the information will be delivered by other means (e.g., on a CD), chances are that the web will be instrumental in letting people know of its existence and its price.

The problem then is how do people behave on the web when they look for information? This translates to: How do people search for information? What can information sellers do to make sure that they are found? While I do not want to provide a complete manual on "search engine optimization"—which today is a dynamic multibillion dollar industry—I find it crucial that information sellers understand its underlying principles. How is information "organized" on the web? Where is this structure coming from if nobody is responsible for building it? What are the basic principles underlying search algorithms? For the information industry these are questions that can hardly be ignored.

Google's PageRank

Who would deny that the word "search" has become synonymous with Google? It has pretty much become the first step in accessing information for most of us. At the time of writing this book, Google controlled about 50 percent of the searches on the web globally. But is Google an information seller? Isn't Google just a search engine while the real sellers of information are distributed on millions of sites on the web? After all, if one needs to pay for the information, the money is sent to these sites. But Google finds these information sources and—most important—ranks them. As I argued earlier, Google is an information seller because it adds significant value to the actual information it delivers to the searcher (decision maker): its *relevance*.[3] Imagine—as is pretty much the case in reality—that a searcher only looks at the first ten hits on Google! The rest is discarded. Isn't Google essentially defining the information market about the topic in question?

Given Google's prevailing dominance over finding information on the world's largest information repository (the World Wide Web), information providers need to understand where Google's rankings come from. A site's rank in a particular search context is supposed to reflect the relevance of its content: the higher the site's rank, the more relevant its content is.

But how can Google measure content for millions of sources in millions of contexts? It clearly cannot be an expert in each content area. It uses many tricks, most of which are proprietary. One of these tricks relies on previous users' feedback. When a user is offered multiple search results he may try a few before finding the right one where he will ultimately spend a larger amount of time. Google can monitor which site is chosen the most from among the possible options, and build this information back in the chosen site's ranking for the next users' benefit. With billions of searches a day this method provides an incredibly powerful way to rank sites for each search query. Another trick to measure relevance is even more fundamental to Google's original success. It is an indirect measure of relevance that is computed from the link-structure of the web. Again, the exact algorithm used is proprietary but the general concept, called PageRank, was described in a scientific paper published by the two young founders of the company—that paper became the basis of Google.[4]

The basic idea is quite simple: if we assume that the flow of surfers on the web is constant (in the sense of being stationary)—similar to the flow of a fluid through a complex system of connected pipes—then the connection structure of the web will have a major impact on how much traffic is reaching a certain site. For example, if a lot of other sites link to an information source then we can assume that this site gets a lot of traffic too. If next we assume that traffic is related to the amount of content on the source, then we can assume that between two information sources containing the same search word, the one with more links leading into it (and hence directing more traffic to it) can be considered "better." In essence, we assume that the "demand" for the source is a good proxy for its quality. To determine incoming traffic even better, one can go further and take into account the number of links that go into the links that end up pointing to the source in question. Or looking even deeper, one can take into account the links that end up in those links linking to the links that we are interested in, and so on ad infinitum. Solving this problem for all the interlinked sites of the web is quite hard. PageRank is an algorithm that proposes a way to do it efficiently.

The main point to take away from the core principle behind PageRank is that the connection structure of the web will play a major role in how each source is evaluated by search engines (by now, pretty much all search engines use an algorithm similar to if not the same as Google's). Since we all rely heavily on search engines to rate information sources, our assessments of information sources will also be heavily influenced by the link structure of the web. Clearly, our acceptance of search engines indicates that it makes sense to rely on the web's link structure to evaluate content.

Now if this is true then understanding the connection structure of the web and the forces that are constantly building it are essential for any information seller. Indeed, if this huge public but decentralized network becomes the "megastore' for data, information, and knowledge, then any information seller needs to worry about how it will be found in it. But beyond its practical relevance, understanding why structure is connected to the quality of content is a fascinating question. It is important to realize that PageRank is a heuristic. It is based on the authors' intuition and it was far from clear that it would work. On the vast network of the web, nobody is responsible for overseeing which site connects to which other sites and why. It is amazing that the decentralized actions of tens of millions of sites end up resulting in a structure that reveals each site's overall value in any search context. In what follows, I would like to help explain why this might be the case.

The Structure of the Web

Figure 6.1 represents the link structure of the web over the earth. How can we find order in such a complex network? Can we talk of "structure" at all? At first glance it does not seem to be the case. If not order visible to the eye, there does seem to be some kind of order on the web, however. Mathematicians, who see the web as the realization of a random graph, characterize it with what they call the "degree distribution."

Roughly speaking, the degree distribution measures how many sites have a specific number of other sites connecting to them. If one were to represent this as a picture it would look something like figure 6.2. The horizontal axis on the figure measures the number of in-links that a site could have, while the vertical axis measures the number of sites for a given number of in-links. The scales are logarithmic so it is quite tricky to read them. On the vertical axis, for instance, 1 corresponds to the totality or 100 percent of the sites and as we go down on the scale the number of sites (or more precisely their proportion) goes down quickly. For example, 1e-09 at the bottom of the scale corresponds to 1 in a billion sites, which is 0 for all practical purposes.

How to read the figure then? Take the dot on the upper-left corner of the plot. It roughly corresponds to 2 in-links (by the horizontal scale) and to almost 1, meaning the totality of the sites (by the vertical scale). In other words, the figure suggests that almost all sites have less than two

Figure 6.1
A map of the World Wide Web.
Source: http://newmedialiteracies.org/blog/2008/09/maptacular.php

links pointing to them. As we move southeast on the figure the proportion of sites with higher and higher numbers of in-links decreases drastically. If you look at the lower-right corner of the plot, what you see is that the proportion of sites with over a thousand in-links is much less than one over a million. In fact, as the number of sites is finite it becomes harder and harder to express small proportions. As a result, the end of the plot becomes confusing: for example, the proportion of sites having between 1,000 and 100,000 in-links seems to be the same. This is because we are talking about a single site in this whole range. The dashed line corrects for this imperfection. It represents the line on which the dots would line up if there were an infinite number of dots. In other words, while figure 6.2 applies only to a subset of the web—specifically to the link structure of sites within Hungary only—the entire network's structure would look identical with the dots lined up on a straight line. Mathematicians say that "the degree distribution follows a power law."[5] In the case of the web, if one were to look at out-links it would again look very similar. The main

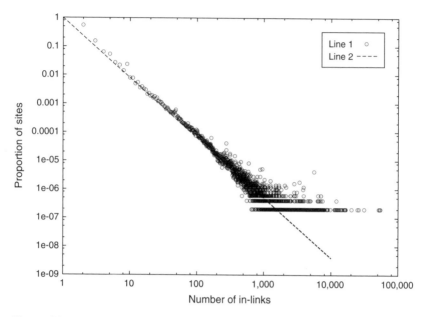

Figure 6.2
The in-degree distribution of the Hungarian web. The horizontal axis represents in-degree, while the vertical axis measures the proportion of nodes with a given in-degree, both on logarithmic scales.

pattern is then clear: *the vast majority of links point to a tiny proportion of the sites.*

Why is this interesting? First, it makes Google efficient. It basically confirms that—if we believe that a higher number of in-links reflects more relevance—there are indeed large differences across sites on this measure and this allows Google to easily discriminate among sites. But there is a second reason why this pattern is interesting. It raises the question: what causes sites to establish links this way? Remember that the PageRank concept is based on the strong assumption that a higher number of links means "better" content. But is it true that sites tend to establish links to higher-content sites? A number of scientists have asked this question in recent years and have developed models that try to reproduce the power-law degree distribution of the web.[6] Most of these models, however, are statistical in their nature and typically ignore the important fact that sites are run by people who follow economic incentives when they decide between connecting or not connecting to other sites. Also, most of the models manage to explain the degree distribution of in-links but would typically be silent on the number of out-links. One of the mysteries of the web is: why do in- and out-links follow almost identical degree distributions?

The Market for Links

To address these puzzles, I and one of my colleagues at UC Berkeley decided to develop a set of models that treat websites as economic agents.[7] In each model, sites were assumed to be different from one another with respect to their content: some had high and others had low content. We also assumed that content is a proxy for the public's interest in the site. A higher-content site was associated with the site's higher ability to earn money from the traffic flowing through it. Finally, sites were allowed to establish links to one another at some cost. In one set of models that we called "reference models," we assumed that sites establish out-links to reference other sites, thereby increasing their own content (similar to scientists referencing each other's work to increase their arguments' credibility). In another set of models, called "advertising models," sites purchased links from others for a fee to increase traffic to their own site. In this latter case, the sites' profit came from sales of links to other sites as well as from the traffic flowing through their own site (i.e., the sales of their own content).

Solving these models revealed a fascinating pattern. Figure 6.3 shows a simulated network from our models. The circles correspond to sites and the arrows correspond to the links between them. The size of each circle reflects the content of the site with a bigger circle meaning better content. If one looks at this network no structure stands out. It seems just as confusing as figure 6.1 (although it clearly represents a much smaller network). But let us now arrange the sites in increasing order of content on a circle as is done in figure 6.4. The complex structure now becomes simple. Sites with a lot of content (large circles) typically have high number of in-links and low number of out-links and the reverse is true for sites with a small amount of content (small circles).

These results confirm the hypothesis behind the PageRank concept, namely that more in-links are an indication of better content. If sites are economic agents then they will establish a link structure that conforms to this pattern. The models also teach us other interesting things. The exact distribution of links (the famous degree distribution that network researchers are all worried about) depends, of course, on the specific distribution of content across sites. However, we could show that in case of a power law distribution for in-links, the out-links also follow the *same* distribution, as is the case for the web. The funny thing is that this structure is very

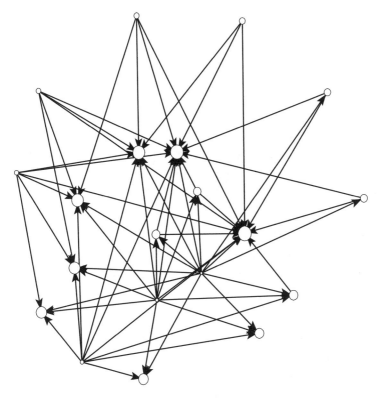

Figure 6.3
An equilibrium network of sites with different contents as measured by the size of the circles representing them.

robust to the type of model we used: it applied to our reference models as well as to advertising models.

The case of the advertising model is particularly interesting. In this model sites allow other sites to buy links from them for a fee, which they set themselves. A site with a high level of content and therefore high revenue potential was found to set a high price for a link; the reverse was true for sites with low content levels. This makes sense: a site with high content does not want to drive traffic away from itself, rather it tries to benefit from the traffic that arrives to it. The reverse is true for a low content site: as it cannot earn a lot from the traffic flowing through it, it is better off selling this traffic to other sites. In essence, we observed that sites specialized: the low content sites became advertisers who sold the traffic going their way to other sites. In contrast, the high content sites

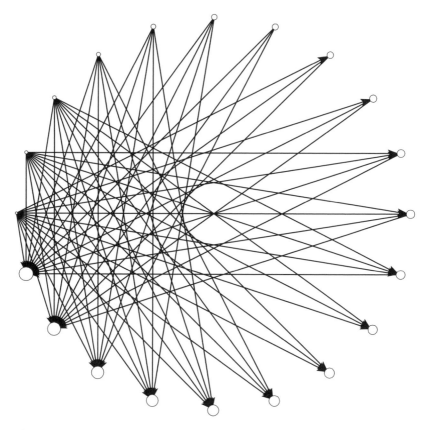

Figure 6.4
An equilibrium network of sites with sites arranged on a circle in increasing order of content.

ended up buying a lot of links to leverage their content with the high traffic generated to their sites. This type of allocation is quite familiar to marketers and economists in the context of traditional (broadcast) media, such as TV, radio, magazines, and so on. It is called the Dorfman-Steiner rule, which states that firms making higher margins typically spend more on advertising than their low-margin competitors. In the context of a network medium, spending more, however, means buying more links.

In sum, Google's PageRank works because its underlying search philosophy seems to be well grounded in economic theory applied to the owners of information sources. Google's founders had the right intuition in interpreting the web's complex structure. More generally, it is fascinating that the vast repository of information on the web "self-organizes" by freezing into its link structure the demand and supply conditions for information.

One question remains. Understanding Google's PageRank concept, can a site influence its position in the ranking? Or, can it "fool" the search engine into believing that it has high content when it doesn't? The answer is yes, and given the importance of search rankings a whole industry has emerged to help sites optimize their ranking. Search engine optimization (SEO) often represents a line in most firms' online marketing expenditures. Some of these practices are questionable and indeed aim at fooling PageRank. For example, if one creates a so-called link farm (a large set of bogus web pages that are all linked to a target site) then this could artificially inflate the target site's in-links and, in this way, its perceived importance. But such practices can be identified by Google's search technology and allow it to "punish" cheaters. The case is similar for other tricks that sites might be tempted to consider using to fool the search engine. However, there are legitimate practices as well to increase a site's ranking (e.g., obtaining links from established content sites), and hence the importance of understanding the basic mechanisms that drive the rankings.

Search in Real Time

Search in general remains a key area where one can expect spectacular improvements in the future. As the World Wide Web slowly becomes the dominant network medium, with an ever-increasing proportion of all digitizable content on it, search remains a top priority for every member of the economy. One of the key areas of development, for example, is determining how to adapt search algorithms to real-time dynamic content. This is not a new problem. In the last decade, blogs—online journals edited in real time based on their readers' comments—have proliferated on the web.[8] In 2010 there were about 200 million blogs. However, as the limits between blogs, microblogs, and social networks tend to disappear, the amount of rapidly changing web content is exploding. Twitter's success highlights how "real-time" content has become important for Internet users.

For search this is a real problem and poses the same challenge as the exploding number of websites did fifteen years ago. How can one find one's way in this growing jungle of ever-changing information? In contrast to web pages, blogs are dynamic objects that change by the minute and become obsolete just as quickly. If I am interested in an emerging opinion with respect to a certain topic, then I cannot use comments that were made a few days ago. This is typically the lead time that traditional search engines need to index the World Wide Web. Imagine that you are a stockbroker who heard a rumor and want to see if people have picked it up in the last few hours. You cannot rely on traditional search.

In the early 2000s, several startup companies (e.g., Technorati, Feedster, and Blogdigger) jumped on the opportunity to provide search capabilities on the blogosphere. Some of them have already disappeared and, of course, Google has invested heavily in finding ways to efficiently search the blogosphere. Its advanced search for blogs is quite efficient and even allows one to search according to how recent an update is. Given that it is a trade secret, I am not sure whether Google's blog search algorithm uses the link structure among blogs. Research suggests that this could certainly be useful: Dina Mayzlin and Hema Yoganarasimhan from Yale University and UC Davis have noticed that blogs tend to link to other blogs in the same category.[9] This is quite surprising, because it seems as if they are driving their audiences away from their own sites. The authors' argument is that through this linking blogs can signal to their audience their capability of finding the "breaking news" that the audience seeks on the blogosphere. The authors show that as a result of this incentive, better blogs (meaning blogs with better news-breaking capabilities) end up having more in-links from other blogs. This is a similar pattern to the one we found for websites. It seems that the "economics of link creation" works similarly in a variety of contexts on the web. More important, it results in similar link structures that can be exploited for efficient search.

Humanlike Interfaces

Type ALICE into Google and among the first ten hits you will find the site of the Artificial Intelligence Foundation. If you click on it, you end up on a page with a beautiful cartoon figure in the left corner talking to you. Alice's hair is brown, she blinks, and she moves her head and eyes—with a certain charm—her face wandering after your cursor on the screen. You really have the impression that she is interested in knowing what you are up to next. The page has a few cool links that may teach you more about Alice and you will also find that for a few dollars you can build your own prototype character to support your website. Clicking you will also have the chance to engage an "award-winning version of Alice." You can have a conversation with her about anything and she will reply pretty much as a human, although once you've asked her a few questions you will realize that she doesn't "know" much. In fact, she doesn't really know anything. After about two minute it is clear that Alice is just a database of frequently asked questions. But this is precisely the point. All that is humanlike in Alice is her appearance, yet for two minutes she could impress you. Are similar humanlike interfaces relevant for the distribution of information?

Let's take another example closer to information markets. In October 2006, Microsoft introduced a new search engine, called Ms. Dewey. The launch was intended to be a viral marketing campaign to promote Microsoft's search functionalities. Ms. Dewey was different from existing search engines in that it created the impression of interacting with a real person. The implementation was based on a simple idea. When you loaded the site an actress (played by Janina Gavankar) stood in front of you on the screen. She was quite funny while she was waiting for your question, even showing some boredom from time to time. When you asked the question, she made a comment that seemed to be related to the question, although—as for Alice—it was pretty much pulled out of a database. The real information you were interested in showed up later as a list of websites just like a traditional search engine would produce. Arguably, Ms. Dewey was a timid attempt to improve search interfaces but it is surprising how effective it was at making one feel you were interacting with a real person—at least for a short period of time.

Ms. Dewey did not last long. In January 2009 the msdewey.com website was closed. And so far, no major information provider has invested in a similar interface. Instead, the industry continues to use the traditional, mostly text-based interfaces. But is it possible that in the (not so distant) future information will be presented to us by virtual people or "avatars"? Can avatars become the checkout counters of information sellers? Does the interface matter that much, anyway? Don't rational decision makers worry about the content of information rather than the way it is presented to them? These are timely questions because avatar technology has become quite advanced. High-quality computer gaming interfaces are easy and inexpensive to produce. As a consequence, there is an opportunity to better "format" the information. The quality of this information formatting can become a relevant competitive advantage for information vendors.

"The Media Equation"

One should not underestimate the relevance of "social interactions" in the context of search or any information transmission. Knowledge transmission in particular often requires feedback and interactivity. This is not a problem with regard to technology: sequential search theory and other techniques can help refine a search or allow the cross-referencing of different information sources. Rather, the problem relates more to marketing. When a search fails we are annoyed. Yet if you carefully listen to a conversation, the information exchange is hardly very efficient and it mostly consists of noisy "back-and-forth" between the speaking partners—something like:

"Have you seen the knife?
"Beg your pardon?
"Where is the knife?
"Which knife?
"The one with the black handle.
"I think it is in the sink.
"I already checked; it is not there.
"Ah, how about the table, did you look?"
. . .

While unsuccessful searches on a computer quickly annoy us, we mostly don't mind this situation in real life. Why is this so? The answer is simple: because we are inherently social creatures. We have been designed by millions of years of evolution to interact with humans and we are good at it. In fact, there is plenty of evidence that people treat interactions with every possible medium or information source as a social interaction in the human sense. The idea is not that people dislike technology in general, but rather that they dislike technology that does not behave as humans do.

In the mid-1990s Clifford Nass and Biron Reeves, two researchers in the School of Communications at Stanford University (Palo Alto, California) did an interesting study. They replicated virtually all social psychology experiments that psychologists tested on humans but instead of humans they used various types of media. The media varied from computers to such simple things as a smiley face painted on a wall. They wrote up their findings in a book entitled *The Media Equation*.[10] The title is very telling. Their surprising conclusion was that people treat the media as they would treat other people. They develop feelings (affection, anger, anguish) toward them. People behave socially with media, in other words, they respect the rules of social interactions such as, for example, politeness. An experiment revealed, for instance, that subjects rate the performance of a computer higher when the computer asks for ratings about its own performance than they do if another computer asks for the ratings. In other words, people tend to be "nice" to the computer that they judge, just as when they provide direct feedback to someone. Other experiments showed that people respond to humor proposed by the medium appropriately by engaging in humor themselves, as if they faced a person. They develop judgment, which would be based on well-ingrained social prejudices. In one experiment, subjects systematically rated computers with a female voice as being less intelligent than the same computers using a male voice, replicating old-time social prejudices against women. Indeed, one of the most interesting findings is that when people are asked whether they think they act socially with media, they clearly believe that they do not. The evidence shows that they do and it actually takes quite a bit of effort to suppress this social behavior.

The Media Equation provides very important insight into interface design. More generally, it raises the question: what will be the ultimate interface to the web? Will it be the PC, as it is today? Are we going to use a keyboard or a mouse to enter queries and answers as we do now? Even touch screens and mobile interfaces are mostly based on text-based information or pictures. Existing interfaces are not very well adapted to social interactions.

Avatars

There is a domain, of course, where humanlike interactive interfaces flourish: computer games. The gaming industry has showed astonishing growth in the last decades. Despite the tech recession after the 1990s, the sector has been growing at around 10 percent per year to surpass Hollywood and every other entertainment sector. Some of the largest technology firms have invested massively in the industry. Giants, such as Microsoft or Sony Corporation spend fortunes (in the order of $ billions) to come up with new generations of their gaming platforms. It is money well spent. For example, while the gaming division is only one of Sony's hundreds of subsidiaries it has been responsible for a large part of the corporation's operating profit. Some of the best programming talent is attracted by independent game developers who compete fiercely and spend billion-dollar budgets to create games that are capable of using the new platforms' speed and graphics potential.

As gaming increasingly moves onto the Internet, it is important to realize that developments in the gaming industry have far-reaching implications for the web or any other area where interactivity plays an important role. Those who are leading the current technology revolution in the computer game industry have always believed so. Over a decade ago (March 6, 2000), Ken Kutaragi, then the CEO of Sony's game unit said in an interview with *Newsweek* about his new game platform, the

PlayStation2: "You can communicate to a new cybercity. This will be the ideal home server. Did you see the movie 'The Matrix'? Same interface. Same concept. Starting from next year, you can jack into 'The Matrix'!"

For those who have seen *The Matrix* (1999, with two subsequent sequels)—in which the entire human race lives unconsciously in a virtual world within a giant computer simulation—this might actually sound a bit scary. Sony and Microsoft, however, may be betting on the future standards of the interface to the ultimate interactive medium, the web. Many believe that within a few years, when the generation of "gamers" grows up and Internet connection is as ubiquitous as credit cards and computers, virtually all aspects of everyday life (shopping, working, studying, going out with friends) will require the use of such an interface. Controlling this interface is equivalent to having a monopoly over the "operating system" of interactive technologies and devices.

How is this relevant to the information industry? As we argued in the introduction, computer games are not information products. However, they have far-reaching implications for the *interface* that information providers may use in the future, and all the more so as games rapidly migrate to the web.

What interfaces should information sellers prepare for? In his science fiction novel *Snowcrash*, which had reached cult status in tech-circles by the mid-1990s, Neal Stephenson presents the modern search engine as an avatar in a "public" virtual world called the "metaverse" (essentially a public computer game that everyone can use).[11] The search engine is actually an advanced interface to the CIA's (by then public) database. Search means logging into the metaverse, meeting with the search engine's avatar, and conducting a conversation with him or her. Just like ALICE, Stephenson's avatar answers questions and points to possible further search directions as would a friend or an advisor in real life. Actually, Stephenson's search engine is even better! When you ask about the weather, a mini-globe representing the Earth appears in front of you with clouds moving around it. You can zoom in countries or cities to find out what the weather is going to look like as if you were "Superman" flying in the skies (or an avatar in a Google Earth application). If Stephenson's vision is technologically feasible, shouldn't information vendors be prepared to present information in such *truly* interactive forms?

Virtual Worlds

The question is all the more pertinent because the world of *Snowcrash* already exists in many forms. In 2010, there were well over a dozen virtual worlds with a combined population that exceeded tens of millions of members. From a technical perspective virtual worlds are computer games that connect their "players" via the Internet in a virtual space. The big difference between traditional computer games and virtual worlds (or metaverses as they are also called) is that, while computer games have very *defined* environments with rather specific objectives, and strict rules on how objects and avatars interact and on how the world looks, metaverses are open platforms with typically no objectives, few restrictions on the environment, and many possibilities to create objects and define ways that these object interact with avatars and each other.

One of the pioneers of virtual worlds, Second Life (http://secondlife. com) was built by a small San Francisco company, Linden Labs. Linden's founder and former CEO Philip Rosedale modeled Second Life (or SL as everyone refers to it)[12] exactly after Neal Stephenson's novel. In many ways, SL is the typical metaverse. It has absolutely no inherent purpose; there is no quest. Members (or "residents" as they are called in SL) can do whatever they want. As in other metaverses, members can *build* things but the SL platform is particularly flexible in this respect: one cannot think of an object that the platform would not allow members to create. Also, objects can be programmed (or scripted) to interact with other objects and avatars in any particular way. Most important, what members build is their private property and they can sell it to one another. This allows members to set up virtually any environment very fast because each element can be purchased on an open market. With these ground rules (or, actually, the lack of them), over the last couple of years a whole "civilization" has emerged on Second Life. The roughly one million regular members[13] represent a dynamic economy with GDP exceeding hundreds of millions of U.S. dollars. Thousands of businesses set up shop in Second Life including many of the Fortune 500 companies.[14] Ken Kutaragi's forecast more than a decade ago was right on target.

By 2010, however, metaverses were struggling. There are a variety of pragmatic reasons for this. First, mastering the gaming interface still remains a challenge for a lot of people. Easy-to-use social networks, like Facebook, represent huge competition for virtual worlds. Second, there is very little experience companies can leverage on how to use virtual worlds for commercial purposes. There are huge uncertainties concerning a variety of issues including: security, copyright laws, taxes, technology standards, and simply standards of behavior. Second Life, for example, had huge problems shortly after its initial growth period when scandals and fraud created bad press and online gambling had to be banned, leading to an exodus of residents and companies. Which virtual world will survive under what technology standard, and what revenue model, is largely an open question, which prevents companies from committing to a public metaverse such as SL. Interestingly, after about half a decade of existence, it is in the business-to-business sector that virtual worlds develop most dynamically, although most companies tend to rely on proprietary platforms to engage with their clients or employees.[15] But beyond these practical issues, virtual worlds may face a more fundamental problem: they are too virtual!

From Virtual Reality to Augmented Reality

As we argued earlier, humanlike interfaces can be really useful to access information and for social interactions. But the interface cannot be a purpose in itself. We still need to interact with reality as much as possible in our lives (in our work and even in our free time). While using avatars to connect remotely with objects and people can be quite powerful, one does not necessarily want to deal with all the complex aspects of an imaginary world when accessing the Internet. Like computer games, virtual worlds are extremely immersive environments, but this also means that they isolate their users from reality while they are on the platform. Consider a simple example: I can follow a conversation with my friends on Facebook using my mobile phone while I am shopping. I can do this because the interface allows me to zoom in and out of the platform, dividing my attention between the real and virtual worlds. But I would challenge anyone to be on Second Life while doing his shopping.

Another aspect of the same problem is that even if the user is prepared to completely devote her attention to the platform, most users want content that is relevant to the real world. Instead of sightseeing in an imaginary city, she might want to deploy her avatar in the virtual representation of a real city using Google Earth, for instance. What virtual worlds lack today is the capability to efficiently import and integrate already existing representations of real-world elements. Virtual worlds are supposed to be filled with content by users. But this is hard work if all aspects of the environment need to be created from scratch. In contrast, while social networks also rely on user-generated content, users have to "fill" a much simpler environment and doing so is much easier.

Increasingly, instead of "virtual reality," people talk about "extended reality" or "augmented reality."[16] This coincides with the explosion of mobile devices and smart phones and the associated location-based services. Augmented reality is an environment in which the real and the digital worlds are tightly connected. Rather than being a single platform, augmented reality represents a variety of platforms and devices that all allow the blending of digital content and virtual elements like avatars with representations of the real world. A weather forecast published on the web can trigger the watering of your garden. The picture of an object taken by your mobile phone's camera can be complemented with information about the object downloaded from the Internet in real time. For example, the picture of an archeological site can display relevant historical data about it. More controversially, the picture of a person can trigger a search on the web and provide personal data about her. Google's Goggles service, introduced on Android phones, recognizes objects like book covers, paintings, and landmarks, allowing instant queries about them. Many of the innovations in virtual worlds migrate to more traditional platforms of the web. For example, Rocketon, a startup company, has replicated location-based social networking for traditional webpages by allowing the visitor of a webpage to post his avatar on the page and interact with other people also looking at the page at the same time. The service turns the lonely experience of surfing the web into a social experience. Many social networks have introduced the trade of digital goods on their platforms using real or virtual currencies.

For the information industry these developments represent a revolution. In this chapter, we concentrated on how these developments will impact channels and interfaces, in other words, on ways in which information can be brought and presented to people. Search technologies have a major impact on how fast information is available, and on how exhaustive and recent it is. However, equally important are innovations that allow information sellers to design new interfaces. Given all the changes on the web, it is hard to predict what interfaces will emerge as ultimate winners for the information industry. A major insight from research, however, is that humans are inherently social creatures when they "consume" information, and this applies even when they interact with unanimated information sources. This insight provides information vendors with great opportunities for differentiation, especially in a context where the web may commoditize information products.

Key Lessons

1. The emergence of the World Wide Web, a free, high-bandwidth, ubiquitous interactive medium, may threaten the core competitive advantage of information sellers whose main competence lies in information

distribution—typically data vendors and the like. Adopting this new technology requires them to come up with an entirely new value proposition.
2. The World Wide Web may also present a major challenge to differentiated content providers who need to compete in an environment crowded with information sources. In particular, information sellers need to understand how to efficiently drive traffic to their websites through appropriate search technologies.
3. Search technologies are in their infancy. There is tremendous opportunity for information businesses to explore new search theories to bring useful information and knowledge to decision makers.
4. Mass interactivity—and Web 2.0 specifically—has a fundamental impact on how information is presented to customers. Computer game technology has an important role in developing customer interfaces. People interact with all media socially.
5. Go and see *The Matrix* (the original film and its two sequels) then read Neal Stephenson's book *Snowcrash* and set up an account on Second Life.

7

Branding Information

This chapter addresses two closely related steps of going to market: branding and communication. Branding and communication are actually quite elaborate topics treated in dedicated textbooks. Our goal here is not to reproduce these texts but to point to the topics' particularities in information markets. In a nutshell, branding is the art of encapsulating complex meanings and connotations in a word or a short fragment of a sentence. Once a formal value proposition has been developed for the information product (see chapter 5) it needs to be translated to a simple form that consumers can remember and transfer to each other. This is the brand: a name representing a promise of valuable customer benefits. The more complex and abstract the value proposition is, the harder it is to transfer its core message in a single word. Marketing communication (advertising in particular) has a key role in this process and typically, the largest portion of firms' communication budgets are spent on brand building.

However, marketing communication also has another, related but slightly more tactical role: "persuasion." Persuasion means: walking the consumer through her buying decision process and along the way, making sure that the product passes each decision step. In practice, this translates to making sure that the consumer is aware of the brand, knows its features, considers the brand, and ultimately buys it. Persuasion may even extend beyond purchase by making sure that consumer satisfaction is sustained during and after consumption. Let's first consider communication's persuasive role in knowledge markets and then address some of the challenges related to branding information products.

Persuasion in Knowledge Markets

Marketers have a general model to describe how consumers decide about the purchase of a product. It is called the AIDA model.[1] AIDA is an acronym. It stands for Awareness, Interest, Desire, Action. Each word represents one stage of the decision-making process. The order of these stages is important. Each stage builds on the previous one in a hierarchy and if one stage is missed it means that the consumer is lost for the firm making the product. First, consumers have to be aware of the product. If they are not, then they will not exhibit any interest in it and will not be able to develop a favorable evaluation of it. Similarly, if consumers are aware of the product, they still have to gather information about it (Interest) in order to be willing to buy eventually. If they don't know the product's key benefits, chances are that they will not prefer it to other alternatives. In reality, for any concrete purchase decision the marketer needs to understand the consumer's sequential evaluation process in much more detail, but AIDA is a good conceptual model of what happens in consumers' minds. Persuasion then essentially means deploying the appropriate marketing "weapons" (advertising, promotion, etc.) in the right order to make sure that the product passes each stage of the customer's evaluation process. The actual weapons and their implementation will be product- and industry-specific but the general principle is always the same.

Is AIDA relevant for the information industry? More important, is AIDA relevant for the sale of knowledge? After all, most information is sold to businesses that have a much more complex and systematic evaluation process. This is even more pronounced for knowledge products. There, word of mouth and personal relationships play a much more important role than advertising, promotion, or other traditional marketing tools. Will advertising ever sell a management consulting service, for instance? Bain and Co., one of the top three strategy consultants of the world had to find out the answer the hard way (see box 7.1).[2]

In the framework of AIDA, Bain's core problem in the 1980s was that in a fast-growing market, it missed the initial, awareness stage of the customer evaluation process. Bain had a great client retention strategy but a lousy client acquisition strategy. Building awareness through word of mouth is a slow process. In a market where most customers are new to the product category, word of mouth is simply too slow to ensure fast enough growth in the face of competition. As mundane as advertising is, when it comes to building awareness it is hard to find a better way.

The key lessons from Bain's story are twofold. First, information markets do not escape the AIDA process and this is even true for knowledge markets that are typically based on strong personal relationships, extensive customization, and word of mouth. Second, information sellers often need to be more creative to find the appropriate weapons to address the AIDA

Box 7.1
Marketing at Bain & Co.

At its foundation, Bain's corporate identity was specifically built around an anti-marketing attitude. Bain believed in and introduced the concept of "relationship consulting." The idea is that the consultant and the client have a strong relationship and work closely together. Instead of spending three months on a project, which ends with a strategy report and then collecting the fees, Bain's vision was to remain with the client for an extended period of time and share the benefits that the project generated. Bain's corporate philosophy was so strong that the industry called the firm the "KGB of consulting." At one point Bain consultants did not even have business cards. The argument was: "if the client does not know the consultant's telephone number then this is not the type of relationship that Bain would like to work in."

There is no doubt that Bain's fresh philosophy of consulting was well received by the market and the firm quickly built a strong reputation that placed it right next to other top strategy consultants. Word of mouth among clients led to a healthy growth of the business. It all went really well until the beginning of the 1980s. Then, Bain started to lose market share and it also received some complaints from its clients. Large, multinational customers were sometimes confused and found that Bain's relationship with their different subsidiaries was quite idiosyncratic.

What changed? Three things. First, and most important, starting in the 1980s management consulting experienced unprecedented growth that lasted until the end of the millennium. Furthermore, this growth came from the adoption of management consulting services by companies abroad. New markets opened in Asia, South America, Eastern Europe, and the Middle East. Some of Bain's new competitors that had not built a strong reputation yet used traditional marketing techniques, such as TV and magazine advertising (see figure 7.1) and sponsoring of sport events, to quickly acquire new clients. In contrast, Bain's growth depended solely on clients' word of mouth, which in an exploding market proved to be too slow and resulted in market share loss.

The second problem was globalization. Many of the most profitable clients were global and worked with Bain in multiple countries or continents. Coordination was key in these projects. Bain's relationship with its clients was local, however, and relied too heavily on individual relationships rather than a relationship with the firm and all of its employees. Business cards would actually have been useful in this environment where a unified firm image and the assurance of the corporate brand are crucial.

Finally, the basic model of consulting changed. Consultants' traditional value proposition was: "we provide smart people to help solve your problem." However, the emerging value proposition said: "we share our worldwide experience with you." This could mean, for instance, that some

Figure 7.1
Competitive advertising of consulting services by Andersen Consulting
©Andersen Consulting

Box 7.1
(continued)

consultants (e.g., experts on a particular topic) would come from far away and would spend only a limited amount of time on the project before moving on and helping another team. Again, the role of personal relationships gave way to corporate relationships.

Faced with these problems Bain quickly reacted and built a coherent firm-wide marketing strategy. It coordinated each office's marketing activity and promoted a worldwide corporate image across them. Business cards not only ceased to be a taboo, they also looked the same across the whole firm. More important, Bain has addressed the problem of building awareness in the corporate world about its services. While it could not simply use advertising, which would have compromised the corporate image, it found other ways to do so: promoting conferences and publishing white papers and management books. As a result of these combined efforts, Bain managed to stop market share erosion while keeping its reputation as a leader in "relationship consulting." Its adverse attitude toward marketing has definitely changed.

steps of their consumers' evaluation process. Bain, for instance, could not consider matching Andersen Consulting's aggressive ad campaigns because it would have compromised the brand carefully built around the theme of "relationship." It had to be more creative in finding the appropriate way to build client awareness. Putting "thought pieces" in the public domain proved to be the right approach.

This second lesson—adapting customer acquisition to the core business—may be even better illustrated by the experience of Ernst & Young's consulting arm in the mid-1990s when it tried to introduce the concept of "retail consulting" to attract small- and medium-sized clients.

This brief history of retail consulting teaches us a nice lesson about communication in information markets. As the client base becomes broader and more fragmented it starts to resemble a consumer market where addressing the first step of the AIDA model—awareness—becomes a challenge. While raising awareness in the community of Fortune 500 companies could be achieved by sponsoring a conference for CEOs (as Bain quickly found out), the same level of awareness in the community of small companies can only be achieved with a broad advertising campaign. Advertising is undeniably the most efficient method to build awareness in a large and diverse population *if* there is a medium where this population can be reached. However, if advertising is not an option (say because such a medium is not available) then the information vendor needs to think hard to find a substitute solution. Ernie (see box 7.2) was one such creative solution that—I think—worked pretty well in the context of the Internet boom.

Box 7.2
Ernie and the Birth of Retail Consulting

In the mid-1990s, Ernst & Young's management consulting arm (today part of Cap Gemini) decided to introduce a new service targeted to small- and medium-sized companies. Called "Ernie," it was a web- and e-mail-based consulting service that a small company could subscribe to for a yearly fee. It allowed the subscriber to ask the firm questions and guaranteed that a consultant would reply with answers within twenty-four hours via email.

The idea was to start a new trend, known as "retail consulting," which would allow for growth outside the traditional market segment of large management consulting firms like Ernst & Young, whose traditional customers were big corporations with complex management problems and deep pockets. In contrast, retail consulting targeted smaller firms with a

Box 7.2
(continued)

less customized service. It leveraged the huge knowledge base that accumulated at consulting firms about broad application areas or industry sectors. Following Ernst & Young's lead, other functional consultants (e.g., former Andersen Consulting—today called Accenture) have also introduced similar services targeted to small clients.

The sales argument behind the introduction of Ernie was quite sophisticated. Ernie was not meant to be a low-quality service that would lead to price competition from small consulting boutiques. It was argued that only a large consulting firm would be able to successfully implement the concept of retail consulting because the background knowledge base required for such a service necessitates large players with the appropriate "knowledge technologies."[3] Such technologies are capable of generating, identifying, and locating information and knowledge from the vast pool of "experience" represented by the thousands of consultants within the consulting firm.

Ernie was a considerable success at its launch with many small companies subscribing to it. Clients were generally satisfied. While they realized that the answers to their questions might not have been very deep, their goal was to receive pointers quickly from a competent person and Ernie delivered on this promise. Furthermore, the service did not attract a lot of competition from lower-end consultants, a major concern of Ernie's opponents. Neither did it tarnish Ernst & Young's reputation as a high-end management consultant in certain domains. Yet, retail consulting as a concept did not really take off and after the 1990s it pretty much disappeared as a concept.

What happened? Did Ernie fail? Not quite. The idea was well received by clients. The problem was related to the cost of serving these clients. Sure enough, the knowledge was there and technology could help leverage it. In the mid-1990s, when Ernie was launched, the Internet had just taken off, and Ernst & Young had invested in a major knowledge management initiative with massive IT infrastructure to tap into the firm's existing experience. But what revenue stream was expected from Ernie? Nothing consequential, as long as it attracted a few hundred (say a few thousand) small businesses. If Ernie were to attract millions of small organizations however, there would be a problem: consultants would need to spend all their time answering subscribers' questions on email rather than attending to their high-margin projects with the large clients. Ernie was not meant to be a new growth engine for Ernst & Young. It was meant to be an advertising campaign to build awareness in the crazy world of the Internet bubble.

In the mid-1990s, the problem was that the high-tech sector was populated with "small" companies that were nevertheless worth hundreds of millions of dollars. They had small staff, little cash flow, typically lost money, and often had inexperienced management. At this stage, these were

Box 7.2
(continued)

not attractive clients for a management consulting firm, which would typically add value in complex management contexts in large organizations
and charge big fees for its services. But could Ernst & Young afford not to
build awareness in this segment? What if one of these small clients became
the next Yahoo! or Amazon.com? Ernie was an easy way to put a foot in
the door for many of these potential clients. In this context, it was a successful communication strategy. However, retail consulting died with the
end of the Internet bubble when this strategy was no longer needed for
client acquisition.

Branding "Unreliability"

Besides persuasion, the second, more tactical role of marketing communication is to "fill" the brand name with meanings and significations
that are consistent with the positioning statement of the product. For example, the brand name FedEx is associated with a reliable delivery service
anywhere in the world. The company's communication department had
to spend millions of dollars repeating the brand's slogan "The world on
time" before the word FedEx was associated with the meanings "ubiquitous coverage" and "reliability," both nicely condensed in the company's
slogan.

What are the relevant meanings that should be communicated in information and knowledge markets, and is there anything particular about
them? To answer this question we first have to ask: what is important to
consumers and what consumer perceptions are favorable to information
products? In fact, we answered these questions when we drew the perceptual map of information markets in chapter 2. Among other things,
consumers certainly evaluate information products along two perceived
dimensions: (1) "independence" (compared to other sources of information) and (2) reliability. An information vendor's service receives better
evaluations when it has an independent perspective compared to alternative sources of information and when it offers reliable information. The
first concept, "independence" (or "uncorrelatedness") does not seem to
pose too many challenges. Communicating that the firm has an independent perspective is very similar to the standard notion of differentiation.
As long as the firm can claim any difference in its methods, perspective,
or school of thought compared to its competitors, communicating it boils

down to the issue of how to do so effectively and creatively in order to cut through the "marketing noise."

Reliability—even though it is a more traditional concept than independence—poses more of a challenge. There is no problem if the firm is a monopolist. As we have seen before, then, it should advertise "reliability" in the traditional way. But being a monopolist is an unlikely state of affairs. Under competition, however, firms may be better off if they sell unreliable information. As we argued in chapter 3, firms selling unreliable information are perceived by consumers to be complements. Consumers tend to buy multiple products and as a result firms can charge high prices. Were firms to claim the reliability of their information, consumers would perceive them as substitutes; they would only buy one product and firms would end up competing by lowering their prices.

For many information vendors these insights do not come naturally. Figure 7.2 shows an ad from a Reuters campaign. This is just one ad from among a number of similar ones, each emphasizing some aspect of the firm's services (e.g., the "timeliness" of Reuters' information, its accuracy, etc.). The campaign was probably meant to achieve a number of things—for example, increasing awareness about Reuters in general—but one of its key effects was to associate Reuters with a number of, ideally, appealing features. This is okay, but clearly, if Reuters is not a monopolist in the financial data vending business, then emphasizing product reliability might not be a great idea.

But does a firm really want to say that its product is "unreliable"? As we saw before, the unreliability of an information product may come from multiple sources. It may come from the firm itself, its methods, the quality of its employees or its data sources, and so on. Clearly, if customers associate the product's unreliability with the firm, this will develop adverse attitudes toward the firm and chances are that sales will be hurt. No one will buy from a lousy information vendor and it is too easy for a competitor to capture the unreliable firm's sales by claiming careful data collection or high quality analysis, or both.

But unreliability may come from sources external to the information vendor. It may come from the unreliability of the available data. No matter how careful the firm is, it simply cannot find better data. This is often the case in emerging markets where the infrastructure for data collection is simply nonexistent. The unreliability of information sources may also be an inherent characteristic of a volatile industry. We have seen before that no one could provide good forecasts for the rapidly changing high-tech

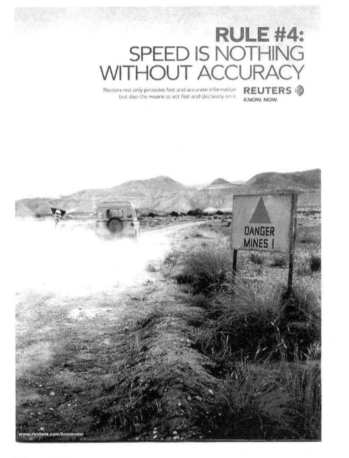

Figure 7.2
Reuters advertising the reliability of information
©Thomson Reuters, M&C Saatchi producer

sector at the end of the 1990s or for the mobile telecommunications industry in the mid-1980s.

The first thing to do, therefore, is to use communication to disassociate "unreliability" from the brand and to associate it with the product category or industry. The core message should not be that "our product is unreliable" but that "everybody's products are unreliable"; that is, "the world is an uncertain place." Some Reuters ads—from the same campaign as the one mentioned before—do a wonderful job in communicating this message. Figure 7.3 shows an example that I particularly like.

**RULE #2
WHAT YOU DON'T KNOW
CAN HURT YOU**

Missing out on the right information can seriously affect your decisions. Reuters offers fast access to more relevant news, plus essential prices and analysis from over 4,000 sources. With 85% of the players in FX and money markets using Reuters to trade, no wonder the top banks choose us. Don't get caught. Go to www.reuters.com/fx

REUTERS
KNOW. NOW.

Figure 7.3
Reuters advertising uncertainty
©Thomson Reuters, M&C Saatchi producer

Positioning Information on the "Shelf"

Advertising your competitors' unreliability is easier said than done at least if one wants to stay within the limits of the law. There are a few tricks however. One of them was unconsciously revealed to me by my wife when, after the birth of our first child, she went to buy a book about childcare. Her friends recommended Dr. Spock's famous text, an undisputed bestseller on the topic. When she left the house in the morning her clear objective was to buy it. When we met again that evening, I asked if she found the book she was looking for. To my surprise she brought out four books (only one of which was Spock's). When I asked what happened she described her shopping experience. Finding Spock's book was easy: a quick inquiry to the salesperson in the bookstore and she was directed to the appropriate section of the store, where half a shelf was devoted to Spock. All around, however, other books on childcare abounded. A quick inspection of the shelves revealed that childcare has a huge literature. This information already created some uncertainty in my wife's mind: was Dr. Spock's really the only book to consider? To answer this question she started to sample the available childcare literature, randomly opening and reading a few lines from the introductory chapters of some of Spock's "competitors." Now the situation became really worrisome. It quickly became apparent that other authors had very different perspectives on childcare. Furthermore, these differences led to a large variance in recommendations on how to deal with particular situations of childcare. Like any rational decision maker, my wife concluded that multiple perspectives needed to be considered and a final solution to a concrete problem needed to weigh the pros and cons of multiple recommendations, each provided by a different expert. Clearly, going with only one opinion is likely to lead to mistakes and a better approach is to consider multiple perspectives. Bottom line: we needed a library on childcare.

An important aspect of this story is that it was the presence of all those other books that triggered the perception of uncertainty in my wife's mind. Did this lead her to not buy the book she originally set out to buy? No. Dr. Spock is definitely part of our library. But a few of his "competitors" are as well. Yet these are not real competitors. If they really were competing with Spock in the traditional sense of "substitutes," then physically placing them next to his classic work in the bookstore would have clearly hurt sales. But rather than taking away sales from one another the simultaneous presence of multiple books actually helped the sales of the whole category. The assortment "teaches" customers about the uncertainty surrounding the complicated topic of childcare, and points to the potential complementarity between competing perspectives.

When my wife told me about her dilemma in the bookstore it quickly reminded me of a marketing problem that I faced in Boston only a year before. At the height of the Internet boom creating new online marketplaces was one of the fashionable ways to set up a new venture. Hundreds if not thousands of marketplaces were launched online, covering many sectors from consumer goods to business-to-business products and services. Triggered by the emergence of mass interactivity, the general idea behind these new institutions was that putting competing products alongside one another would make it easier for consumers to search and compare alternatives. Lowered search costs for buyers would trigger in-creased competition between sellers and lead to lower prices. Lower prices in turn would attract more buyers to the marketplace, which—if it moved fast enough—would end up controlling the distribution of the product category. That was not necessarily bad logic for a business plan.

Information markets did not escape the trend. Forrester Research and some other industry analysts of the high-tech sector (see table 2.3) were approached by a potential startup with the idea of an online marketplace that would feature shorter versions of their full reports on a single web-site. The target customers would be small- and medium-sized companies that could not afford tens of thousands of dollars for a full, customized industry report but would be ready to pay a smaller sum for a less detailed version of it.

The idea received little enthusiasm if not resistance from the informa-tion vendors—which is of course the caveat of all marketplace business plans. In other words, would suppliers be willing to participate in a marketplace that pitches them against each other and decreases their profits? Automatically all the high-tech analysts assumed that being side by side on the same website would commoditize their products and trig-ger increased price competition among them. While this is the underlying logic for most marketplaces, this may not be the case for the information product category. As we have seen in chapter 3, the logic is particularly fallible in the category of industry reports on high-tech industries that are known to be extremely volatile. Knowing their large consumers' be-havior, namely that most of them buy from multiple (sometimes from all) information sellers, should have at least grabbed the imagination of the analysts. As we have seen before, these reports are complements rather than substitutes. The assumption that putting alternatives side by side triggers price competition is only true if these alternatives were substitutes. When they are complements, this is not true and prices are likely to remain high. Furthermore, the fact that the reports are side by side provides an opportunity to "teach" customers about the volatility of this market and, therefore, the need to acquire multiple perspectives. Any individual analyst has little incentive to teach customers about the industry's structure but if they were all present at the same "location," the marketplace could have done the teaching job—just as the bookshelves did for my wife on the topic of childcare. A few pieces of contradicting data about market trends would have quickly convinced buyers that a single report would not tell them much about the future. This marketplace never took off. It's a pity. It may have been the only marketplace that would have been beneficial for seller participants who were supposed to "compete" in it.

Moreover, in today's world of electronic distribution it is almost unavoidable for sellers to compete side by side. A good example is MarketResearch.com, one of the largest online distributors of business information. It is the electronic shelf of over 250 thousand pieces of market research of various kinds from a variety of research firms covering nearly every industry. Buyers can search this large database by subject but they can also peek into the reports to gauge their content. In 2010, there were over two hundred large providers of business information and dozens of so-called aggregators who integrate and package business information originating from many different sources.[4] This setup provides tremendous opportunity for marketing the attributes of "competing" reports through the structure of the information product shelf space. Some information vendors have realized this opportunity early. In 1996, eStats was a small consulting startup specialized in measuring Internet traffic for websites. It published a report projecting online advertising for the next five years. The report compiled the forecasts of many "competitors" and presented all of them in a table (see table 7.1).

Of course, the company did not try to promote its own report comparing it to the others. Rather, the intention was to show how valuable these forecasts were in the first place. Anyone doing online advertising on the Internet in these early days realized the huge uncertainty in the industry. In

Table 7.1
Online advertising revenue projections in 1996 (millions)

Year	1996	1997	1998	1999	2000	2001	2002
IDC	260	550	1200	2000	3300	NA	NA
Forrester	NA	500	1000	1750	4100	5600	8100
Cowles/Simba	236	597	976	1580	2460	NA	NA
Jupiter	301	940	1900	3000	4400	5800	7700
Activ/Media	Na	400	1700	4700	11200	23500	43300
IAB	267	906	NA	NA	NA	NA	NA
Yankee Group	220	630	1200	1820	2200	3800	6500
eStats	175	650	1500	2200	3800	6500	8000
Global Internet Pr	310	NA	NA	NA	5000	NA	NA
Actual	267	907	1900	4600	8100	7100	6000

Source: eStats, PWC

this situation, only *all* of these information sources *together* could provide a reasonable forecast on what might happen. The eStats goal was to teach clients about the uncertainty in the market.

Communication with Multiple Brands

If competition (in the sense of alternative providers) is good for an information seller under certain situations, why not start one's own competition? Imagine that a firm has access to multiple information sources. It can follow two product line strategies. It can pool together and integrate the information from the different sources and introduce the resulting summary as a single, better product. Alternatively, it can keep the information from different sources apart and introduce each of them as a separate information product—maybe even giving them different brand names. Clearly, the integrated product is going to be more reliable and valuable for customers than any of the brands based on a single information source. It is easy to show that in terms of pricing there is no difference between the two strategies as long as the firm is a monopolist and consumers are similar to each other. If consumers are different in their willingness to pay for the reliability of information then the second strategy (keeping the brands apart) may provide more opportunities for price discrimination.

But the real difference between the two product line strategies is in terms of communication. We have argued that for a single firm, it is hard to "teach" consumers about the uncertainty of the environment. There is a lack of credibility when it comes to talking about the reliability of other firms. Furthermore, there is also a general lack of data to support these claims. Could Forrester, for example, provide extracts from a Gartner report to make the point that high-tech markets are hard to forecast? Not really. As discussed, an independent marketplace that distributes all the competing firms' products is one possible solution to this coordination problem. As an independent entity this firm has credibility, just as a supermarket does when it puts multiple brands from the same category on its shelves and claims that its products encompass the largest variety. But what if a firm has multiple brands that—in the eyes of the customer—have nothing to do with each other? This is the ideal setup to teach consumers about the market's characteristics, and in particular, about the uncertainty of the available information. The brands can be brought together in a distribution outlet (a website, a catalog, etc.) where together they can illustrate the range or uncertainty associated with the environment. No product is singled out and all of them contribute to the teaching process.

As they are in the hands of a single firm (a fact not known to customers), the coordination problem is resolved.

Furthermore, the nice thing about this setup is that consumers are not being exploited. At least not really. Consumers would not pay less for a single integrated brand than for the bundle of individual brands as long as they have the same perception about the uncertainties represented by these products. But of course, the whole purpose of separating the products is to change consumers' perception of uncertainty. To the extent that this effort is successful—in other words, consumers' perceived uncertainty increases—firms can increase their prices. Put another way, one can say that consumers are simply better educated about the need to consider multiple perspectives, which is of course the whole purpose of communication.

Communicating with Competitors

Branding and positioning are not just for customers. On the contrary! They constitute the means to build corporate identity and, as such, the brand talks to all market constituencies: to customers, of course, but also to the company's partners and, more important, to its competitors. Strategists often refer to the concept called "strategic posture." It essentially designates the generic way a firm wants to compete with others. It describes the brand as a competitor.

Information markets do not escape this aspect of branding. What message will the branding recommendation outlined so far communicate to competitors? Asked in a different way, how will brand meanings like "independence" and "unreliability" impact competitors? How will competitors react? The news is good. These brand meanings are far from being aggressive and chances are that they will trigger similar strategies from competing firms. Independence is easy to understand. If a firm advertises that it is different from others, that makes everyone better off. This is the basic concept of differentiation. But advertising the huge uncertainty surrounding the environment has a similar effect. On the one hand, rather than triggering price competition among information sellers it makes them complements and leads to higher prices and profits for all firms. If, on the other hand, a firm advertises how reliable its information is compared to others, this firm had better have a real advantage in terms of reliability and this advantage had better be clearly seen by customers. Why? Because under such a branding strategy, competitors have no other choice but to claim the same advantage: high product reliability. Consumers will assume that they need to purchase information from one firm only and this perspective leads to cutthroat price competition among firms, resulting in low profits.

But isn't advertising unreliability in the marketplace just collusion? Aren't competing firms essentially fixing prices? Not quite. First, firms are not explicitly fixing prices. Prices increase because consumers buy multiple products—in other words, demand increases. As long as the message is fundamentally true (i.e., it is not an outright lie) customers will value multiple reports and they will pay according to the value of the information. There could be a concern, however, that firms—while cooperating so nicely in their brand messages—may also be tempted to fix their prices and have even higher profits. True, but the beautiful thing about information markets is that this will not hurt consumers. On the contrary! As we have seen in chapter 3, when products are complements price fixing by competitors leads to lower prices and helps both firms and consumers.

Key Lessons

1. Apply AIDA for your information business and make sure you don't forget to build "awareness."
2. Don't be afraid of advertising the unreliability of your product category. Convince your competitors to do the same.
3. Don't be afraid to feature competing information products on the same "shelf" as long as the products relate to a highly uncertain context (and as long as the information products are independent).
4. Introducing multiple independent brands or building a portal for competing information products can be an efficient method to communicate the unreliability of an information market.

8
R&D for Information and Knowledge

In early 2010, *The Economist* published a special report on managing information, in which it estimated the total amount of information on Earth to be about 1.27 zettabyte.[1] This is an unimaginable amount of information that continues to grow at an incredible rate, leaving far behind our capacity to store it, let alone make sense of it. For example, in retailing, five billion bar codes are scanned every day throughout the world. The largest retail chain, Wal-Mart processes more than a million customer transactions every hour. On the World Wide Web, Google handles about thirty-five thousand queries every second and thirty-five hours of video are added every minute to its YouTube site. It is estimated that the total amount of digital information increases tenfold every five years.

Information technology has exploded the potential for the generation and processing of useful data and information. Information management—helping organizations to store, organize, and make sense of their data—has become a business that is estimated to be worth 100 billion dollars and grow at around 10 percent per year.[2] Suppliers to this industry (HP, Oracle, IBM, SAP, Microsoft, and many others) invest billions of dollars in their data management and analytics capabilities. IBM, for instance, launched in 2009 the new service IBM Business Analytics & Optimization Services to advise its clients on data analysis.[3] The company has four thousand dedicated staff to tailor its in-house methods to the client's analytic problems. IBM has spent billions on buying firms that make business analytics software, the market for which was estimated at $25 billion in 2010. IBM and its peers are at the heart of the information industry. Measurement and analysis is the most fundamental method to create useful information and knowledge for decision making. It can be thought of as the R&D function of the information industry. With the wealth of customer transaction data available, IT-based analysis represents huge opportunities for information vendors.

However, beyond amazing development in data generating and analytic tools, IT has also provided a new platform that completely changes the paradigm of information and knowledge creation. This is of course the web or the phenomenon of mass interactivity. The web is particularly important for the information industry because it is a platform where content can emerge spontaneously. Users uploading content voluntarily ("crowdsourcing") is, of course, one way for this to happen. But what is more interesting is how (social) interaction between users may spontaneously generate content or information, or both, beyond what users consciously upload on various websites. There is a subtle but important distinction to be made between data generated via customer–firm transactions (as in the earlier examples with Wal-Mart or Google) and data generated via customer-to-customer transactions as when users connect to each other and share content on a social network site like Facebook or Twitter. The new opportunity for information sellers is to harness the social interactions between individuals in a community to generate new information or knowledge. In this environment, the information producer can rely on the interactions of thousands or millions of people to create something qualitatively new.

However, interaction on the Internet does not necessarily have to take place among people only. Increasingly, the web directly connects to a variety of data-generating devices whether these are manipulated by individuals (e.g., a mobile phone) or remain inanimate measurement instruments (e.g., street cameras). In another 2010 report on "smart systems," *The Economist* speaks of "the internet of things" to describe the phenomenon whereby sensors can seamlessly integrate the web.[4] Sensors can send and receive information via the network, control other devices, and report their measurements to remote observers. This data flow in turn can be analyzed and turned into useful knowledge. For example, information from the network of street cameras can be aggregated to provide traffic reports. Moreover, an emerging application domain seeks to integrate sensors into social interactions. Sensors can have a "page" on social networks the same way individuals can set up their pages on Facebook.[5] Sensors can feed data streams into the social network, allowing people to interact with the data or make the data part of the conversation between members. A variety of services started analyzing this rich data flow to generate information and knowledge about emerging hot topics, or news on the web, or popular new physical locations of interest to certain communities, and so on, a phenomenon also referred to as "crowdsensing."

The rest of this chapter explores technologies that are all based on the idea of integrating the information or knowledge of large and diverse communities. In his book *The Wisdom of Crowds*, James Surowiecki argues that we underestimate the power of "collective knowledge."[6] He presents dozens of examples where the collective decision of a community outperforms even the best decision of its members. Connecting billions of people practically in real time anywhere in the world makes the World Wide Web an incredible platform for the "wisdom of crowds." How can information and knowledge vendors exploit this platform and harness social interactions to create new knowledge? We will look at four broad technologies to do so: (1) free sources of collectively built content; (2) systems that pay or reward information producers; (3) prediction markets, where people reveal their opinion by trading special securities; and (4) technologies that extract knowledge from the spontaneous interaction of people in communities.

"The Free Encyclopedia That Anyone Can Edit"

Wikipedia, "the free encyclopedia that anyone can edit"—as is advertised on the front page of its website—is probably the most successful example of "user-generated content" on the web, a true embodiment of Web 2.0. It was launched in 2001 by the millionaire Jimmy Wales.[7] Wikipedia is a nonprofit organization living largely off donations that cover the maintenance of its hardware and software infrastructure. Its real asset, however, the enormous amount of content accumulated on the Wikipedia site, is built for free by tens of thousands of anonymous volunteers. The resulting knowledge base is by no means negligible. In 2010, Wikipedia consisted of close to seventeen million articles in over two hundred and fifty languages and it was still growing fast. Beyond sheer size, Wikipedia has multiple advantages over traditional encyclopedias. It exploits the web's html technology that allows anyone to use links to obtain further details on subtopics and link to other, related articles. It is also possible to see each article's edit history, which then highlights controversies and disagreements between subsequent contributors. Each page on Wikipedia is a living document that evolves over time.

The basic paradigm behind Wikipedia—and behind encyclopedias in general—is in sharp contrast with that of Google. In Google's system, access to the world's knowledge happens through *search*. In this paradigm, finding structure is hopeless given the vast amount of information and the endless ways it can be organized. Any particular structure may be irrelevant anyway. Structure depends on context, and what may be the organizing principle behind a given structure for someone today might be outdated for someone else tomorrow. Encyclopedists disagree of course. They believe in an ultimate structure and more important, they believe in some objective definition of quality. Traditional encyclopedias claim quality by relying on *experts*. Faithful to its web origins, Wikipedia proposes a radically different approach by delegating expertise to the decentralized community of people who will ultimately use the knowledge. One could argue that this almost "democratic" process solves the problem of "relevance" and quality, especially if articles are allowed to change over time to incorporate new links and references. The argument also seems to be supported by scientific evidence. For example, a recent paper by a researcher at UC Berkeley showed that the length of articles in Wikipedia is strongly correlated with their quality.[8]

Unfortunately, it is not at all clear that the free and voluntary editing process will guarantee even an attractive structure, forget the "ideal" structure—if it exists. Economics provides endless examples where decentralized decision systems lead to solutions that are ultimately suboptimal for the community that chose them. The history of industrial standards is a good illustration—think of the well-known examples of the QWERTY keyboard or Microsoft's operating system, both of which have been broadly claimed to be of lower quality than available alternatives. Standards are hard to change—this is their purpose. If for whatever reason the wrong standard is picked early on, the community may stay with it forever.

Similar is the case with "quality." Wikipedia's history provides plenty of examples where quality was compromised. One of the obvious quality issues is perpetuated by the so-called Wiki-vandals. These are people who, for no apparent reason, load the site with false or even obscene content. From a technical perspective, screening this content out is not too difficult. The edit history of each article is stored and previous versions can be easily restored. The problem is that someone needs to spot this undesirable graffiti. In practice, Wikipedia's small group of voluntary administrators is doing this cleaning job. So far, they have managed to keep the site remarkably clean. But what if the site grows much bigger? Is it going to be possible to keep it free of rubbish in the future?

Wiki-vandals have no apparent reason to put false or rubbish content on the online encyclopedia. As Wikipedia grows, however, it faces another threat, coming from so-called scrapers who have a definite incentive to modify the content in a questionable way. The idea is simple. We have seen (in chapter 6) that Google's PageRank algorithm (which strongly reflects the value of a website) "rewards" sites that have in-links from other, well-connected sites. As Wikipedia grows and its popularity increases (i.e., more and more people refer to it on the web), it becomes very valuable to have a link from Wikipedia for any site. In this way, the site in question boosts its own PageRank in association with the site-specific search words. This can then result in a large increase in the site's traffic. If the site sells advertising, it can free ride on Wikipedia's popularity to do so. Scrapers have an easy time exploiting this opportunity as they can freely add content and links to Wikipedia. While they are being hunted down by the administrators, this may take time during which advertising revenues keep accumulating for them. Furthermore, hunting scrapers is harder than hunting Wiki-vandals. The latter's objective is to be visible, which means they are easy to find. In contrast, scrapers have an incentive to hide in the jungle of information.

"Inclusionists" vs. "Deletionists"

But the fundamental problem with Wikipedia lies elsewhere. If a few administrators are the ultimate judges of what is rubbish and what is not, aren't we back at the same old system where a few "experts" define the structure of knowledge as opposed to its users? This situation could then lead to biased information or the overrepresentation of some views over others. In this case, the situation is even more sensitive because we have no way to verify or trust the expertise of the administrators. In fact, we don't even know who they are. Who decides, then, what is quality? For example, does one have the right to correct an article written about oneself? This issue came up in 2007 when one such person, Daniel Brandt, realized that Wikipedia contained an entry on him that he did not agree with. He corrected the page but unsolicited editors kept adding content that Brandt needed to keep under tight censorship, a task that became harder and harder as new edits were added to the article by the hour. At some point he asked for the removal of the entire entry, which in itself raised a number of questions about the credibility as well as legal standing of the online encyclopedia. Wikipedia is based on the principle that, essentially, no one is responsible for the validity of the content and no one owns the copyright to it. The article on Daniel Brandt was not withdrawn at the time (although when I checked recently it did not exist). He, however, has started Wikipedia Watch, a site that exposes some of these obvious controversies with respect to the content of the popular online encyclopedia.

It still remains that, at the end of the day, the ultimate judges of content are the site's administrators. Based on what *principles* will they ensure the quality of content on Wikipedia?

With the growth of the site, this problem has taken an institutional dimension. A 2008 article in *The Economist* exposed a bitter fight between "inclusionists," who argue for relaxing the strict editorial criteria to keep contributors motivated, and "deletionists," who would prefer Wikipedia to be more selective in its content.[9] In particular, deletionists are worried about the imbalance between the detail devoted to trivia (e.g., Pokemon characters or George W. Bush's nicknames) and the neglect of important topics such as, for example, the solidarity movement in Poland. The battle between the two camps concerns the formal "rules" that decide whether articles should be kept or deleted. These rules, in turn, rely on measures that relate to the quality of other information sources. So, for example, a reputed international journal counts as a high-quality source and so does *Playboy* magazine, and if the subject is mentioned in these outlets it increases the likelihood of being included in Wikipedia. The irony is that one of these measures relies on the number of Google matches. This in itself is an acknowledgment that, as opposed to rules set by a few individuals, the global "market" for content (reflected in the web's link structure) should decide on what quality is.

Of course, irrespective of the actual measures used, the very idea of using rules to decide on the universal quality of information is hopeless. The process is highly susceptible to becoming political and subject to all kinds of games among the privileged decision makers. More important, the more the process is subject to strict rules and "wiki-lawyering" (as the increasingly cumbersome policing process is referred to) the more hurdles this means to potential contributors. As inclusionists rightly point out, the population of contributors is likely to decrease. Evidence seems to support them. Competitors of Wikipedia (in particular, other online encyclopedias such a Citizendium or Scholarpedia, which rely on "certified" experts or a thorough peer review process, or both, to ensure quality) are nowhere close in size and popularity.

Despite all of these problems, Wikipedia has emerged to be a wonderful source of content. If your search falls on a Wiki article you are likely to find structured and comprehensive content that traditional search engines would have a hard time providing. In fact, in a world dominated by search engines, Wikipedia's persisting success may come from the fact that we still prefer information presented to us in a comprehensive book format rather than as a collection of web links. Nevertheless, the debate is far from closed on what the most efficient way is to produce knowledge from a broad user base. Let us explore a few other approaches.

Folksonomies

If we were to contrast different R&D technologies for generating information and knowledge, then Wikipedia is a good example of what I would call a "knowledge creating" technology while Google's approach, based on search alone, is what could be called "knowledge exchange." In the context of the web, the difference lies in the effort that is needed to create and process the information received. Imagine that—as it plans to do—Google makes all human knowledge searchable on its site. Then, by definition, one could find in the output of a search result all the information that is compiled in any Wikipedia article. However, the processing of the collection of sites that Google would list—each containing a fragment of the relevant content—would be quite difficult. The searcher would need to summarize and weight this massive amount of information even if PageRank would be of significant help. In contrast, all this work would already have been done for the searcher on the Wikipedia article.

What if there was a compromise between these two extreme ways of organizing the vast amount of knowledge on the web? A variety of sites (see, e.g., www.delicious.com or www.connotea.org) propose organized systems of links sorted by various topics without involving experts and without asking their members to explicitly create content. They achieve this by asking members only to "tag" the links that they found interesting. Tagging means adding a few descriptive keywords to the link describing its content. Members can use any word as a tag and as many tags as they want. This process, a simple technology in which a categorization system is spontaneously created by millions of people through tagging, is called a "folksonomy." Folksonomies are particularly interesting when nonverbal content needs to be organized. A few tags allow the efficient categorization of images for example, a task that would be quite challenging otherwise. YouTube, Google's video-sharing site, for instance, uses tags to make search possible among the millions of videos available on the site.

How tagging creates a consistent structure is still a mystery, but it was found that from the enormous amount of possibilities people tend to converge on a narrow set of words for describing content. Typically, the most commonly used tag would be used twice as much as the next most commonly used, and so on. In other words, the top few descriptors pretty much represent how the vast majority of people describe the content in question. This pattern is similar to word usage in natural languages. It is also related to the reference link structure of web pages that we described in chapter 6: plotting the rank of the words versus their frequency follows a power law (see figure 6.2).[10]

Folksonomies are yet another example of a simple technology that can generate organized knowledge from a large number of simple information sources by relying on the power of many interconnected individuals. Their power comes from the fact that they constitute a compromise between search-based knowledge generation and explicit knowledge creation through editing.

Questions and Answers

In 2005, Yahoo! started a service called Yahoo!Answers where you can be part of a community that allows you to ask an open question addressed to other members about any subject. Members volunteer their answers. The advantage is that you can formulate a complex question and obtain an "intelligent" answer to it. In other words, your question will be interpreted by a real person. Remember the AI agent ALICE quickly disappoints because her answers are too mechanical, often missing the essence of the question. Having a real person at the other end makes the processing of answers much easier. With the emergence of Web 2.0, question-and-answer sites seem to be undergoing a renaissance. In 2010, so-called social search was claimed to account for about 4 percent of the global search market.[11] Besides the many startups (e.g., Fluther, Quora, and the market leader Answers.com), some of the large players also decided to launch their Q&A services. In 2010, Google was reported to have purchased Aardvark for $50 million and Facebook introduced Facebook Questions to its then-five-hundred-million user base.

But the reliability of information obtained this way is far from being of high quality. As long as the community is small and focused (such as, e.g., Quora's, a startup fashionable among Silicon Valley insiders[12]) people seem to take questions and answers seriously. However, when the site expands, respondents seem to become disengaged and often churn out rubbish. It turns out that in large communities the answers are not much better than ALICE's. Q&A services resemble social networking—a sort of advanced chatting—rather than real knowledge creation through the "wisdom of crowds." Q&A sites resort to various methods to remedy this quality problem. Usually, they try to identify experts in specific subject matters. The methods either use some form of feedback or explicit search for expertise voluntarily posted on social networks. But the problem does not always come from the answers; often the questions don't make much sense either. So far, no one has figured out a good solution.

Paying for Content

The systems that we have explored so far—they are often summarized by the term "crowdsourcing"—have the common characteristic that contributions are voluntary and there is no ownership of content. This prevents these systems from benefitting from the power of markets. The best mechanism for judging quality is via a pricing system. Like any market, information and knowledge markets only work if ownership is properly defined and people have proper incentives. Then valuable transactions are likely to occur. How could we modify existing systems to achieve this?

One solution would be to pay the contributors. The idea is very old and dates back to 1714, when the British government established the so-called Longitude Prize that offered a cash prize for a simple and practical way to determine the position of ships at sea. For information markets, the same model has been figured out for a web-like medium way before the World Wide Web's ubiquitous success. When talking about virtual worlds in the context of interfaces, I mentioned Neal Stephenson's science-fiction novel *Snowcrash*. In Stephenson's metaverse, a single data source (the former CIA database gone public) is the basis of all information search. The novel describes in quite a lot of detail how content is generated on this universal search engine. The source gets updated on a voluntary basis by anyone who wants to add anything to it. So far, this is similar to Wikipedia. But the key difference is that contributors are earmarked and they are paid based on the usage of the information they provided. In fact this payment system is similar to that of any business where content is created spontaneously but it is extremely difficult to forecast what people will like. Music—in fact, all artistic content—is produced this way. The artist is paid for each copy sold. Similarly, advertising is paid for on a per-viewer basis. Such a system preserves the decentralized, spontaneous nature of content creation while it provides proper incentives to the contributors.

The model described in *Snowcrash* was introduced in 2008 by today's dominant search engine, Google. The project, called "Knol," is based on Wikipedia's original principle: anyone can add entries on any topic, although the original contributor has ultimate control over what remains in the article. No universal experts are involved in judging quality and content. True to Google's individualist philosophy, it is a voting system that decides which content is of high quality. Moreover, a remarkable aspect of the model is that Google shares ad revenues with the authors. Popular articles can earn more for content providers.

Despite all these innovations, Google's Knol service is not terribly successful. At the time of writing this book and well over two years after Knol's introduction few people even know about it. This is in sharp contrast with awareness about Wikipedia. But why is this so? Part of the answer is timing. It is hard to introduce a comprehensive knowledge service in the presence of Wikipedia and its 17 million articles.[13] Another explanation may be that Google underestimated the "social rewards" of content contribution. Wikipedia contributors' pride in their voluntary work is part of the success of the popular online encyclopedia. But still, Knol seems to have all the desirable features of a proper information market. How can it do so poorly? Moreover, Knol is not the only "pay for content" service that Google has experimented with. In 2002, well before Yahoo!Answers, Google introduced one of the earliest Q&A services, called Google Answers. People could offer a "bounty" of up to $200 for someone to answer their questions and could even add a tip of up to $100 if they were satisfied with the answer. Google kept 25 percent of the bounty in addition to a small fee for each question. In 2006 the service was shut down for lack of interest.

Why did Google's pay-for-content experiments fail? My conjecture is that the fundamental reason is that both Knol and Google Answers were superfluous. The web is in essence a large information market already! As we have seen in chapter 6, the link structure of the web is a decentralized voting system for the best content. It ensures the participation of literally anyone using the Internet. Is there an incentive to create good content? Of course! Such content is likely to become popular and generate a lot of traffic on the corresponding website that can then be turned into revenue in a variety of ways (by selling products or advertising, e.g., or by simply bringing fame to the person who created that content). In essence, today's web, where search is dominated by Google, is not very different from the giant information market described in *Snowcrash*.

The point is that among the many models based on user-generated content that the web proposes, the successful ones will need to rely on some sort of payment/compensation system that is tightly linked to the usage and quality of the content. Such a market system is the only way to ensure that the relevant content or structure will emerge on these decentralized knowledge platforms. Besides Google, another example of such systems, which seem to work pretty well, are "prediction markets."

Prediction Markets

In 1988, the business school at the University of Iowa started an experiment. They set up a market where the securities traded were linked to the outcomes of a variety of political elections. The Iowa Electronic Market (IEM), as it is called, is open to anyone who wants to participate. Traders can buy and sell futures contracts of many sorts based on their beliefs about what might happen in a particular election. For example, during the last presidential campaign, you could buy a contract that would pay you $1 if Barack Obama won the election. If this were not the case, you would not get anything. The price you are willing to pay for a contract like this reflects your belief about the likelihood that Obama will win. The market price then reflects the market's *aggregate* belief that Obama will be the next president. For example, at 67 cents, the common wisdom is that he has a 67 percent chance of winning.

This example is only one of the two popular contracts that you might see on the IEM. It has the notable feature that its payoff does not depend on the proportion of votes that the candidate manages to obtain. The other widely used contract on the IEM pays according to this proportion: say it pays a dollar for each additional percentage point in the popular vote. Then, if the candidate ends up getting 30 percent of the popular votes, you would earn 30 times $1, or $30. At 35 percent of the popular vote, you would get $35, and so on. Here, the price of such a security reflects the market's estimate of the proportion of votes that the candidate will get. If the price is $28 then the market's expectation is that the candidate will receive 28 percent of the popular vote.

In both cases, through its market mechanism, the IEM "produces" useful—in fact very useful—information about uncertain future events. Furthermore, as markets do in general, this information is based on the joint and disparate perspectives of many people. But wait a minute! Don't we already have well-established methods to obtain this information? We indeed have one: the poll. It also aggregates information from many different people. If the poll is done correctly, the participants are a "representative sample" from the entire population. This is important as this is the population that is going to vote. Presumably, people know what they will do. In contrast, the IEM consists of a relatively small number of (in IEM's case, a few thousand) people, who certainly aren't representative of the voting population: most of them are male and come from Iowa. They certainly do not predict their own behavior in the market when they buy or sell stock on IEM.

The obvious question is: how well does the IEM predict elections? Well, it seems that IEM does better than polls—not just occasionally better but systematically better. To explore the performance of IEM, an early study involving IEM elections between 1988 and 2000 was conducted.[14] It was found that in 75 percent of the cases (596 polls), the IEM market price provided a more accurate forecast on the day a poll was released than the poll itself. This is a pretty impressive performance. More recent research shows that prediction markets beat polls not because their participants have better information but because they are better at incorporating information from all sources, including the polls.[15] Markets do not anticipate changes in voter sentiment, rather they react to the release of polling information, albeit very quickly.

The IEM experiment is by no means isolated. IEM is an early example of prediction markets, which are also called "decision markets" or "event futures." Like other markets, event markets have been around forever. After all, IEM is not very different from sports betting. But these markets were relatively few in number. The World Wide Web has changed this. Given IEM's early success, prediction markets keep multiplying. Table 8.1 provides a few other examples based on a survey by two professors at Stanford University's Graduate School of Business.[16]

Among these examples, the Hollywood Stock Exchange (HSX) is another popular market. It trades securities tied to opening-weekend performances, awards such as the Oscars, and any other forecast related to the motion picture industry. A notable difference between HSX and IEM is that the former uses play money only. Yet its performance in terms of accuracy is still impressive. In 2002, for example, HSX correctly predicted thirty-five of the forty big-category Oscar nominees. In fact, Anita Elberse, a marketing professor at the Harvard Business School, has shown that HSX forecasts are the best forecasts among other available alternatives.[17] Interestingly, many of these alternatives include polls of experts (famous producers, actors, and directors).

Figure 8.1 illustrates the performance of HSX in forecasting opening takes for almost five hundred movies between 2000 and 2003. Not only is there a strong correlation between the HSX market price and the movies' opening take, but also the line that is closest to all points on the plot for the data almost perfectly predicts the true outcome. The fact that HSX uses play money only seems to suggest that incentives do not need to be extremely high for these markets to work. Even though it uses real money, IEM is not that different from HSX in this regard. It does not allow people to take positions exceeding $500 dollars.

Table 8.1
Examples of prediction markets

Market	Status	Focus	Typical turnover on an event ($US)
Iowa Electronic Market	Run by University of Iowa	Small-scale election markets for U.S. elections	Tens of thousands (limited to $500 positions)
Tradesports	For-profit company	Trade in a rich set of political futures, financial contracts, current events, sports and entertainment	Hundreds of thousands
Economic derivatives	Run by Goldman Sachs and Deutsche Bank	Large-scale financial market trading in the likely outcome of future economic data releases	Hundreds of millions
Newsfutures	For-profit company	Political, finance, current events, and sports markets; also technology and pharmaceutical futures for specific clients	Virtual currency redeemable for monthly prizes
Foresight exchange	Nonprofit research group	Political, financial, current events, science and technology events suggested by clients	Virtual currency
Hollywood Stock Exchange	Owned by Cantor Fitzgerald	Success of movies, movie stars, awards, including a related set of complex derivatives and futures. Data used for market research.	Virtual currency

Source: Reproduced from Wolfers and Zitzewitz 2004

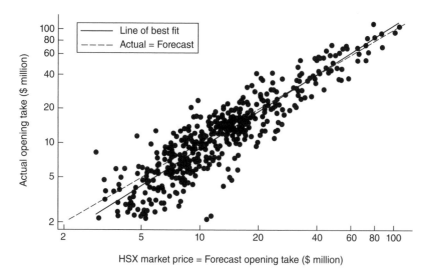

Figure 8.1
How well does HSX predict movie success?
Reproduced from Wolfers and Zitzewitz 2004

Nevertheless, some prediction markets function as for-profit private enterprises and trade up to hundreds of millions of dollars. Economic Derivatives—a site run jointly by Goldman Sachs and Deutsche Bank—is one such market. It trades securities tied to official releases of economic data.

Table 8.1 also suggests that prediction markets seem to work for a large variety of seemingly unrelated contexts. The applications seem to be limitless. This is exactly what the Department of Defense thought in 2003. One of its research think tanks, the Defense Advanced Research Project Agency (DARPA), decided to launch a Policy Analysis Market that would allow forecasting events with political significance. Among the possible candidates figured hypothetical events such as "such and such political leader is overthrown by a given date," "a terrorist attack in a given city," "war in a certain country," or a variety of future economic indicators for foreign states. The proposal was finally dropped because of the ensuing public uproar. Critics accused the government of selling "terrorism futures."

The aftermath of the DARPA project is one of the best illustrations of how well prediction markets work. Somewhat cheekily, Tradesports .com, an offshore betting site, launched a security that would pay $100 if DARPA's chief executive, Admiral Poindexter, would leave by the end of

2003. In their 2004 paper, Wolfers and Zitzewitz nicely document how fast the market price adjusted as soon as news about the affair reached the public.[18] At the beginning, the price of the security was around $40, estimating Poindexter's departure at 40 percent. The first news hit the market around lunchtime on July 31, 2003. It referred to credible Pentagon sources about a probable resignation. The market reacted within minutes, jumping to $80. As no news reached the market for weeks, after this date the security slowly decreased to $50. On August 12, Poindexter issued his letter of resignation, setting his time of departure to the end of the month. In response, the market quickly rose to a closing price of $96.

Securitization on Event Markets

The preceding examples illustrate how efficient prediction markets are at *aggregating* the publicly available information in the market price. Finance theory has reflected this for a long time in the context of financial asset prices, but it is now becoming clear that many aspects of finance theory can be applied in totally different domains, from economic forecasting to market research and politics. So what else can prediction markets learn from finance?

One lesson is that prediction markets do not necessarily have to limit themselves to simple contracts like the ones we have discussed. Just as finance has seen the birth of a variety of securities (e.g., options, hedges, etc.), prediction markets can also be innovative on this front. The benefit is that we can learn much more about the event in question than its probability of happening or its mean (in the case of forecasting, the percent votes earned by a candidate). For example, take a contract that pays according to the *square* of the percentage vote that a candidate gets. The market price of this security would reveal the market's expectation of the value of the square. Then, combining the traditional contract that pays linearly and the one that pays according to the square of the percentage vote, we can estimate the variance of the percentage vote.[19] This is a good measure of how certain the market is in its estimate of the percentage vote. Clearly, beyond the estimate, its reliability or uncertainty also represents important information. But one does not need to stop here. You could go further and design a contract that pays $1 if the percentage vote is exactly 48 (say between 47.5 and 48.4 to be precise). Then, the price will reflect the probability of this happening. Issuing the same security for other percentage values would allow you to plot the entire expected distribution of the vote. While such detailed information may not be relevant, prediction

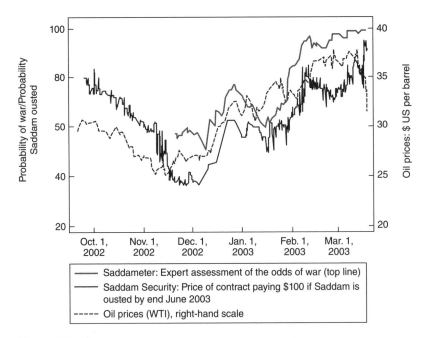

Figure 8.2
Relationship of prediction market data to other relevant variables
Reproduced from Wolfers and Zitzewitz 2004

markets have tremendous power in generating information about future uncertain events.

Even more interesting is how well prediction markets' forecasts connect to other information sources. Data reported by Wolfers and Zitzewitz provides strong empirical evidence. Figure 8.2 shows, for example, how the price of a contract offered on Tradesports.com that paid $100 if Saddam Hussein was ousted by the end of June 2003 moved in tandem with oil prices and experts' opinions (the so-called Saddameter). If we assume that an Iraqi war affects oil prices—a safe assumption—then the figure suggests that war increases oil prices by about $10. Using economic indicators and election data, Wolfers and Zitzewitz report similar patterns for a variety of other contexts where related variables seem to move together with prices on prediction markets. There is evidence, for instance, that futures connected to George W. Bush's election moved together with major stock exchange indices.

Looking at figure 8.2 one might still say: "sure, but in order to measure the relationship between war and oil prices we had to wait months to have enough data to estimate the effect." Not quite! One could have issued two contracts, with both contracts' payoffs linked to the (unknown) future price of oil. One contract, however, would have paid the payoff if Saddam were ousted while the other would have paid if he remained in power. The purchase price would have been refunded in case the owner of the contract lost the bet. Then, the difference between the market prices of these contracts could have been interpreted as the effect of Saddam's ousting on oil prices. In other words, beyond predicting events, prediction markets are also useful for estimating the *relationship between events*. And all this in real time! But one needs to be careful interpreting these patterns. The tandem movement of prices for oil and the Saddam security does not necessarily mean that one causes the other. That interpretation comes from our assumption. As such, the information we generated with this special contract could be thought of as testing the hypothesis that one event causes the other. It remains true that prediction markets are powerful tools to generate information.

Given all this positive evidence, you may wonder why prediction markets aren't more popular. Well they are! In early 2009, I tried to make a complete survey of prediction markets, thinking that this was a "new thing" and so a survey should be easy to do. It quickly became evident that this was not easy at all. Prediction markets are all over the place in the United States as well as abroad. Beyond public markets, like the ones in table 8.1, there are many proprietary ones. Wikipedia featured an article on prediction markets, and even listed a "prediction market portal" for a while, which unfortunately missed some markets.

Prediction markets have also conquered the enterprise. HP, Intel, Siemens Microsoft, Google and Yahoo!, among others, have all been mentioned as experimenting with prediction markets to improve their internal decision making. These decisions cover a variety of contexts—from production scheduling, product sales forecasting, and forecasting the probability of meeting a deadline, to gauging the latest technology trends. Setting up additional applications, whether private or public, has become easy. At least half a dozen commercial prediction markets also provide application development and consulting services. Well-known companies, such as Eli Lilly, Abbott Laboratories, Arcelor, and many others are listed among their clients. Prediction markets seem to be everywhere.

However, one of the serious hurdles to setting up events markets is regulation. These markets are essentially betting markets and as such they are subject to laws on gambling, which (depending on the states) can be very restrictive and cumbersome. The issue is so important that dozens of famous economists published an article in *Science*'s policy forum to encourage regulators to lower the legal barriers for building such markets.[20]

Information Bubbles

Like financial and other markets, prediction markets are not always perfect. They raise a number of questions, to which their short history does not yet provide fully satisfying answers. People have shown, for example, that traders are not perfectly rational.[21] It is well known that people overvalue small probabilities and undervalue near certainties. This psychological aspect of trading is common knowledge in financial and betting markets as well. It basically means that for events with these characteristics, prediction markets may not provide very reliable information.

Also like other markets, prediction markets are not guaranteed against bubbles creating prices that are not associated with real event probabilities. Indeed, a few such bubbles have been documented on political prediction markets. They did not last very long, however. In fact, finance theorists argue that bubbles are much less likely on prediction markets than on their financial counterparts. This is because, as opposed to financial markets, they typically do not impose restrictions on short selling. Furthermore, trades generally represent small amounts, so it is unlikely that informed traders—who would potentially break the bubble—would be cash constrained. All these factors make the likelihood of bubbles much smaller.

Some also question whether prediction markets provide an opportunity for easy manipulation. As the cash traded is typically small (or may even just be play money) someone might be able to easily manipulate prices by placing unreasonable bets. Such attempts were registered on election markets, for instance, when eager supporters placed large bets on their favorite candidates. But these manipulations cannot last for long because they provide increased opportunities for reasonable traders to make money. Unreasonable bets quickly draw a large number of reasonable traders in the market and this usually corrects the anomaly. Manipulation can also originate from the market administrator. This problem was raised in the context of the DARPA project. What if the government learned from the so-called terrorism futures that the risk of a terrorist attack was very high? Clearly, it would act on the information and so change the future probability. Therefore, it would be difficult to trade securities of this type, because traders would not have enough incentive to trade. Theoretically, this problem can be solved. One could introduce contracts that are contingent on government action, but clearly these types of events are tricky for creating corresponding securities.

The liquidity of these markets may also represent a problem. Markets only work if there are a large number of traders with different perspectives. As such, it is critical to attract many participants. With the proliferation of markets this might not be a trivial marketing problem. But the fact that gains in existing event markets are relatively small or nonexistent suggests that people participate in large part for the thrill of betting rather than to pursue economic gains. Nevertheless, in the case of small markets, such as corporate markets, for instance, there is evidence that it is not trivial to keep people interested in participating. Google, for example, uses information markets to forecast the likely performance of its innovations. It also sells a variety of "fun" securities that are only meant to sustain interest for the market among employees.

Finally, it is also worth mentioning that prediction markets seem to be remarkably consistent across each other when they offer the same security. Furthermore, they are also consistent between different securities issued about the same event. It is extremely unlikely, for example, that a contract offering a dollar if a candidate wins the election costs 60 cents while another contract providing a cent for each additional percentage of the votes has a price of 45 cents. Economists call this "would-be" situation an arbitrage opportunity because it would allow someone to make money for free by trading across markets. For the same reasons as in financial markets such arbitrage opportunities are very unlikely.

Prediction Markets Everywhere?

Will prediction markets dominate the information industry? Will they replace traditional market research, expert analysis, and other well-known techniques that have been developed to understand the world around us? I believe that the exact opposite will happen. These traditional methods will not be replaced by event markets, but they will be solicited even more by them.

First, it is not clear that the current boom of public prediction markets will continue. You are probably convinced by now—as I am—that prediction markets provide extremely valuable information. I believe that most of the time, this information is more valuable than the profit generated by running the markets. The real business is in selling the information generated by the market. In fact HSX and some other private markets try to do this. But public markets cannot really benefit from the information generated. The information itself is public and it is reflected in the prices. Without being able to internalize the knowledge revealed, chances are that the rush to this new industry will slow down, at least as far as public event markets are concerned.

In contrast, I think that the corporate event markets will likely flourish. Here, the information can be used to generate huge profits for the firm running the market as it learns key information. This information remains in the firm (just as corporate information is confidential). It can be readily used for future strategy setting or resource allocation. For example, Innocentive, a subsidiary of Eli Lilly, set up a prediction market for employees to figure out which newly developed drugs will obtain FDA approval.[22] This knowledge is critical for a pharmaceutical company and has a major impact on its resource allocation decisions. In the experiment, Innocentive used six drugs, half of which were known in advance to have been accepted by the FDA while the other half were known to have been rejected. As soon as trading began, prices quickly revealed which drugs were successful.

If the future of event markets will be in the corporate or private domain then it is also easy to see that traditional ways to generate information will not disappear at all. Consider market research. It asks customers about their needs, preferences, and decision-making process. This information can only originate from customers. It certainly cannot be dreamed up internally in the firm by employees, at least not in a firm that is "market oriented." This is what half a century of marketing has taught us. In other words, an internal prediction market cannot replace traditional market research. Quite the contrary!

For a prediction market to work well, participants have to have a way to gather relevant information about the events that constitute the basis of the securities. There is evidence that securities based on events about which no public information exists trade poorly on the market. Traders quickly understand that unless they have some inside information they have no chance of winning. For example, at the time of the election of the new Catholic pope in the Vatican in 2005, contracts on Tradesports on the likely identity of the future pope generated little trade even though the event was of central interest for the public and was generously covered in the news. This is because the vote was held completely confidential by the Vatican. In contrast, in a company, a prediction market can do a wonderful job by asking employees about the likely success of a product because it can integrate many considerations *in addition to* market research (e.g., appropriateness of allocated company resources, competition, etc.) It certainly cannot replace market research. Prediction markets are knowledge-generating technologies, not data-generating technologies. They interpret the data but do not generate it. Their potential for knowledge creation in organizations is enormous.

Extracting Information from Online Communities

In July 2005, Rupert Murdoch purchased Myspace.com for 580 million dollars. What he got is a website, where people can create a personalized page with their favorite pictures, music, and videos, connect to their friends, and spend time chatting. At the time of purchase, MySpace had twenty-five million users.

A half decade later MySpace is considered to be old news. Although its membership base climbed to hundreds of millions of users, in 2008 it was overtaken by Facebook. After a rapid decline, in June 2011 it was sold for less than $40 million. Today's successful social networks, such as Facebook, LinkedIn, and many foreign social networks, can boost multimillion membership bases, high valuations, and huge traffic. The Korean Cyworld, for example, claims that one third of the country has a personalized page in it. Similarly, most Internet users in Hungary have a page on IWIW. Also, as mentioned earlier, these traditional social networks are not the only online communities on the web. Online computer games, like the popular *World of Warcraft* or *Grand Theft Auto*, where millions of avatars play in a virtual space, are also de facto communities. Metaverses like Second Life and blogs with a dedicated theme also represent vast communities where people interact very intensely.

Communities—whether they are online or not—are a natural social phenomenon. They always existed. The difference is that in online communities the interactions between members is recorded. This represents a goldmine for information production. Online communities can be considered as real-time market research outlets. Before the web, if one wanted to learn about the content generated in a community (e.g., a political opinion, product preferences, or a scientific discussion) one had to go offline, survey the community, or hope that some published output (e.g., a newspaper, book, or music recording) would result from the members' interactions. Today, the online platform allows constant monitoring of the content generated by users. Furthermore, this can be done by data-mining software because the user-generated content is stored in digital form on the community platform. Of course, there are privacy issues and these are not to be taken lightly, but the possibility to analyze the content generated by an online community is very real.

For example, if I wanted to learn about the musical tastes of teenagers, I could crawl through Facebook and analyze the music posted on the site by the corresponding demographics. I could discover trends and differences across geographies and identify subgroups, the same way I would if I were to run a large-scale market research off line using survey methodology. The online version of the methodology might involve having a person randomly surf on Facebook's vast network of members. However, it could also use sophisticated software to surf instead. This methodology is called "Netnography" by online market researchers in reference to the combination of terms "ethnography" and "Net." Netnography essentially consists of content analysis of online content.

Netnography and other data-mining methods applied to social networks may not only be used to generate market research information. They can also be useful to capture conversations and debates in scientific communities or any other social forum where content emerges spontaneously via the interaction of members. The technology is in its infancy (today it is mostly used by firms to quickly react to emerging negative word-of-mouth in the customer base), but it represents tremendous potential for the information industry.

One does not even need to analyze content to extract information from the members of social networks. How they are connected already reveals a lot about them. In social networks, members explicitly reveal their connections to other members by making them their "friends." These connections constitute a huge graph that may be analyzed to reveal clicks and communities within which information can flow relatively easily. Furthermore, analysis can also reveal particular members who are central to these subcommunities either because they hold them together or because they act as an information hub among members. These members can be particularly important for spreading word-of-mouth information, for example, and for this reason are of particular interest to marketers. By targeting them with marketing messages, the hope is that word of mouth about new offers can spread faster in the target population.

Analyzing the connection patterns in large communication networks (called "social network analysis" or SNA) has grown to become a multibillion-dollar industry.[23] It does not reduce to the analysis of Internet social networks but can be extended to all kinds of communication media. Traditional telecommunication services (voice or text messages) or an email service can also be subject to SNA. A critical amount of communication (e.g., "x amount of calls per week") can be defined to be a connection between two subscribers and allow the construction of a complex graph of connections among the multimillion-user base of the communication service. In turn, this graph can be analyzed to find communities and identify the most influential members within it. During the first decade of the twenty-first century dozens of startups have worked to develop advanced techniques to perform such analysis efficiently.

Communities also represent a goldmine to test new ideas by gathering feedback in real time. The Business Insider (TBI), a new online magazine founded by Henry Blodget, a former Internet stock analyst mentioned in chapter 4 is set up to revolutionize business news by constantly testing a variety of content pieces on its site.[24] When a certain topic catches interest (this is monitored and identified by software), TBI journalists jump on the topic and cover it in depth attracting visitors to the site. In essence, TBI relies on its reader community to define worthy topics to explore for them. TBI is a good example of a "real-time" information-generating technology. Social networks—and increasingly their real-time versions such as Twitter—represent the most up-to-date sources of relevant news. More and more often social networks beat mainstream media in revealing breaking news as, for example, in the case of the 2008 earthquake in China's Sichuan province.

In his 2003 book *Smart Mobs: The Next Social Revolution*, Howard Rheingold draws the contours of a revolution where loose virtual communities are taking over the social infrastructure of modern society.[25] He claims that "smart mobs" are spontaneous (can emerge any time in any context), adaptive (can easily accommodate change), efficient (they are self-organizing, inexpensive, and objective driven), and can represent tremendous power (can overthrow governments, boycott trade, or engage in a deadly war). Rheingold provides many examples, positive and negative, and shows how Internet technology has provided a new platform for a fundamental social change in modern societies. His analysis mostly concerns how our societies will evolve as a result of this technological revolution. A related consequence is the fundamental change in how information will be produced. Today, as we experience the explosion of virtual communities (people with common objectives or interests connected by technology), we need to realize that information and knowledge creation will shift from traditional data generation and analysis to technologies that help us discover and extract the *collective knowledge* of millions of interconnected people.

Key Lessons

1. There are two broad views on how to capture and integrate user-generated information. "Deletionists" rely on experts or coded rules to select "quality" from the vast content provided by users. "Inclusionists" are agnostic about "quality" and rely on search technologies to make sure that any content can be found and its relevance be defined by market forces.

2. In any case, successful, decentralized knowledge technologies using the web should rely on an appropriate incentive system to tie the value of content and the reward for it to the demand generated by it.

3. Prediction markets are efficient at integrating knowledge from diverse sources of decentralized information. They represent a huge opportunity for organizations seeking to implement efficient knowledge management systems.

4. Online communities such as social networks, blogs, or other platforms where people exchange and collectively generate content represent a goldmine for information producers. "Netnography" (online content analysis), social network analysis, and software that can elicit real-time feedback from connected people all represent technologies to analyze and interpret collectively generated content from large communities.

9

Conclusion

Roughly fifty to one hundred thousand years ago, the evolution of the human race suddenly underwent a discontinuous change. Archeologists call this short time period a "cultural revolution" because it is the first time that evidence of "culture" (worked stone tools) appears in archeological data. After this "event," the development of the human race proceeded very rapidly. Human cooperation became much stronger and more sophisticated in literally all aspects of life. Proper societies took form. Major innovations, from construction to agriculture and weapons were quickly developed. Abstract domains such as art and religion emerged.

One of the mysteries of this cultural revolution is that it is not related to a significant increase in brain size, as is the case for all previous milestones of human evolution. What then triggered this sudden change? What happened fifty thousand years ago? We are not entirely sure but most probably, the primary cause of the cultural revolution was the sudden appearance of language. Communication no doubt existed before as it also exists in other species today. But human language is different from any other natural means of communication that we can see on our planet.[1] It is orders of magnitude more efficient. Beyond naming objects it allows the development of abstract concepts, which are necessary for the creation of what we have called "knowledge" throughout this book: the understanding of causal relationships between patterns in the vast amount of data around us. Suddenly, this knowledge not only could be created but also easily transmitted to the next generation, which then developed it further to create new knowledge. In this way a good idea coming from a single member became available to all others, who then built on it and came up with more ideas, and so on. With the advent of language, the speed of human development considerably increased forever. From that point, the development of the human race meant the *social* development of ideas as opposed to the biological development of the species.

A key feature of human language is that it is extremely efficient at connecting the members of society. Coming closer to today and to the context of modern societies, we cannot ignore the effect of major communications innovations in the development of our civilization. These innovations were not brought to us by evolution, as happened with language, but were invented by us. But just as language did, they have all led to a quantum jump in connecting people. Gutenberg invented mechanical moveable type printing, which led to an explosion in knowledge dissemination—multiplying connections across subsequent generations. Wire telecommunications was probably the next revolution in connecting people and making geographic distance almost irrelevant. Similarly, the invention of broadcasting with the use of radio waves forever changed our notion of distance. Today, a similar breakthrough is happening: the Internet. It allows millions to interact with each other, sharing voice and text but also pictures, video, and other rich media.

But the World Wide Web is much more than a communications medium. After almost two decades, it is turning into a "knowledge medium" where new content emerges from users' collective contributions. Increasingly, what we call Web 2.0 is a collective, organic, evolving knowledge source that is being built by all of us and shared by all of us. Constant innovation finds new ways to harness human interactivity in online markets, collectively built knowledge sources like Wikipedia, blogs, social networks, and location-based services. New business models are incorporated in older platforms as, increasingly, social networks dominate the scene but constantly incorporate many applications developed independently (think of the trade of virtual goods on Facebook or its Facebook Places service introduced in 2010).

What is amazing is that the content generated in Web 2.0 is instantaneously available to everyone anywhere at virtually no search cost. Modern search engines help us find anything in this vast ocean of information in seconds. It is becoming conceivable that all human knowledge will be on this medium in no more than a decade. Not so long ago, Google announced a project to make all printed books searchable on the Net. Music and multimedia content will follow. I strongly believe that these developments are extraordinary compared to all other improvements of technology that have occurred continuously throughout human history.

In its special report on smart systems, *The Economist* writes: "Economic value, having migrated from goods to services, will now increasingly move to data and the algorithms used to analyze them. In fact, data, and the knowledge extracted from them, may even be on their way to becoming a factor of production in their own right, just like land, labor and capital."[2]

In this book, I have highlighted how the emergence of new technologies, in particular, the World Wide Web, may affect the information industry. Given the speed of development in this domain, it is likely that many of my speculations will be soon outdated or even proved wrong. My goal, however, has been to describe the fundamental forces that govern information markets. These forces will not change and understanding them may help decision makers face the many changes brought by future technological developments.

Notes

Introduction

1. See Dhebar 1995.

2. See Cool, Harford, and Oppenrieder 2005.

3. Wikipedia and Alacrawiki.com. It is difficult to come up with hard numbers because official statistics do not exist for this category. The information industry—as defined in this chapter—does not have a Standard Industrial Classification (SIC) code.

4. Popper et al. 2002.

5. Shapiro and Varian 1999.

6. These two, demand-driven aspects of the proposed definition for *information products* have been advanced by Jensen 1991.

7. See Foray 2006 for an excellent discussion on the differences between information and knowledge. In particular, Foray points out that, on the one hand, while knowledge can be codified it requires cognitive effort (learning) for its reproduction. Information, on the other hand, can be reproduced through simple duplication.

8. As an example, consider the consulting industry, a well-defined component of the information industry. Consulting has had one of the largest systematic growth rates in the services sector—over 15 percent on average for the last thirty years. Other sectors of the information industry, including financial information sellers, database vendors of various kinds, market research firms, and industry analysts, have also seen double-digit growth rates in the last few decades.

1 Is There a Market for Information?

1. The famous economist Kenneth Arrow was the first to explicitly describe the special characteristics of information when it is considered as a product or economic commodity. See Arrow 1996 for a good summary of his basic arguments.

2. Of course, the firm is unlikely to sell the information to a competitor. In fact, it might buy the report on the basis of exclusivity. We will briefly address this issue when discussing information-selling formats in chapter 5.

3. See Gillespie 2007 for emerging challenges of copyrighting in the digital goods context. In chapter 5, we will also see how information sellers can deal with limited illegal sharing of information across consumers.

4. There is a large literature in finance dealing with information revelation through trade and its consequences (see Admati and Pfleiderer 1986, 1988, 1990).

5. Grossman and Stiglitz 1980.

6. "Shortage of Prophets," *The Economist* 368, no. 8332 (July 12, 2003): 72–73.

2   Decisions and Information

1. See "Number Crunch," *The Economist* 363, no. 8276 (June 8, 2002): 70.

2. Coy 2008.

3. Elstein 2001, B1.

4. See Milhench 2003.

5. With asymmetric sellers one would reach the same conclusions as long as the difference in reliability is not too large between them. In the case of large differences in reliability, the market outcome is quite simple: the firm with much higher reliability drives the low-reliability firm out of the market.

6. See Larréché and Weinstein 1988.

7. Violini and Levin 1997.

3   Competitive Pricing of Information

1. See Zuckerman and Buckman 1999.

2. In 2007–2008, further consolidation in other segments of the information business caused Reuters to merge with The Thomson Corporation to form what is known today as Thomson Reuters.

3. I also developed a formal economic model to see if mathematics confirms these ideas (see Sarvary and Parker 1997), but mathematics is difficult to trust in this case because the assumptions always drive the results.

4. The theory also claims that under complementary information, competitive information prices should be even higher than the price set by a single information seller who is a monopolist. In one version of the experiment, we have checked this hypothesis and found strong support for it as well. A full transcript of the results is available in Christen and Sarvary 2007.

5. When the information sources are correlated, one also needs to take into account this correlation in the weights. See Winkler 1981 for an extensive treatment of this problem.

6. Psychologists have studied the extent to which people follow Bayes' rule when they forecast events and have found various anomalies in the use of priors (see, e.g., Kahneman, Slovic, and Tversky 1982 for a good summary of these findings; and Ariely 2008 for a more recent and easy-to-access review). In particular, on the one

hand people sometimes ignore prior information (e.g., base rates have been shown to be systematically ignored), but on the other hand people sometimes give overly large weight to their prior and fail to update it as new information is revealed to them. These mistakes represent a fascinating topic for psychology, but are less relevant in the context of information markets where information providers and buyers are experts and generally more "rational" in their forecasts.

7. See, for example, "Bayes Rules," *The Economist* 378, no. 8459 (January 7, 2006): 70–71, reflecting on the scientific evidence to date.

8. Medical diagnoses are particularly erroneous, and this is well documented. For a good (and fun) review of the topic, see Makridakis, Hogarth, and Gaba 2009, in which an entire chapter is devoted to the history of medicine.

9. See Young 2008.

10. There are exceptions. According to consulting folklore, Xerox hired three major management consultants to assess the strategic impact of Kodak's entry in the copier business. The consultants were supposed to come up with independent assessments.

11. A detailed analysis of this problem can be found in Sarvary 2002.

12. This example has been adapted from the seminal paper by Banerjee, "A Simple Model of Herd Behavior" (1992). See also Bikhchandani, Hirshleifer, and Welch 1992 for another classic paper on the topic.

13. If the rumors are right only 55 percent of the time (only slightly better than the 50 percent prior), the probability that the 99 independent rumors are all wrong is $(0.45)^{99}$, a tiny number.

14. Surowiecki 2005.

15. Klein and Majewski 1994.

16. See Schmidt 2010.

17. To be fair, in the Madoff case, some investors have done their homework and have even taken on themselves to be the whistle blowers by sharing their private information with the authorities. Too bad the authorities repeatedly ignored their warnings.

18. See Bulow, Geanakoplos, and Klemperer 1985 for a similar argument on accommodating a new entrant in an industry.

4 Why Information Sellers May Lie

1. A more complex issue is that forecasts might actually change the truth itself as a self-fulfilling prophecy, an issue that may also be of great concern to buyers of information.

2. Makridakis, Hogarth, and Gaba 2009.

3. See Sasseen 2008. See also "Restructured Products: A Beleaguered Industry Looks to Reform Itself," *The Economist* 386, no. 8566 (February 9, 2008): 72–73; "Downgraded," *The Economist*, 392, no. 8641 (July 25, 2009): 68. And see Tait 2010.

4. See "Badly Overrated," *The Economist* 363, no. 8273 (May 18, 2002): 75–76; "Free the New York Three," *The Economist* 363, no. 8273 (May 18, 2002): 13–14; "Exclusion Zone," *The Economist* 366, no. 8310 (February 8, 2003): 71–72; and "Let Go of Nanny," *The Economist* 366, no. 8310 (February 8, 2003): 17.

5. See "Downgraded," *The Economist* 380, no. 8486 (July 15, 2006): 62–63.

6. See "The Wages of Sin," *The Economist* 391, no. 8628 (April 25, 2009): 76.

7. See, for example, Wolinsky 1993 and Emons 1997 on the subject.

8. See Tait 2010.

9. See, for example, Chaffin, Michaels, and Silverman 2002. Academics have also studied this issue. Relevant academic articles on the subject include Michaely and Womack 1999; Hong and Kubik 2003; and Morgan and Stocken 2003.

10. Hong and Kubik 2003.

11. Michaely and Womack 1999.

12. Hong and Kubik 2003.

13. Lamont 2002.

14. Ottaviani and Sorensen 2006. See also Lichtendahl and Winkler 2007.

15. Ottaviani and Sorensen 2006.

16. Ibid.

17. Lamont 2002.

18. Chevalier and Ellison 1999.

19. Hong, Kubik, and Solomon 2000.

20. Ottaviani and Sorensen 2006.

21. See "Garbage in, Garbage out," *The Economist* 335, no. 7917 (June 3, 1995): 86.

22. Gentzkow and Shapiro 2006.

23. DellaVigna and Kaplan 2005.

24. Ajami 2001.

25. Franken 2003; Coulter 2003; Goldberg 2002; Alterman 2003.

26. See details in "Americans Spending More Time Following the News: Ideological News Sources: Who Watches and Why," Pew Research Center for the People & the Press, September 12, 2010, http://people-press.org/2010/09/12/americans -spending-more-time-following-the-news.

27. See http://en.wikipedia.org/wiki/Silvio_Berlusconi#Business_career.

28. See "Fit to Run Italy?" *The Economist* 359, no. 8219 (April 28, 2001): 15–16; "An Italian Story," *The Economist* 359, no. 8219 (April 28, 2001): 21–24.

29. See http://en.wikipedia.org/wiki/Rupert_Murdoch#Building_News_Corpora- tion as well as "The Murdochs and Sky: Patience, Rupert," *The Economist* 397, no. 8707 (November 6, 2010): 43.

30. Mullainathan and Shleifer 2005.

31. See, e.g., Graber 1984.

32. See Hayakawa, Hayakawa, and MacNeil 1990.

33. See, e.g., Severin and Tankard 1992.

34. The Pew media survey mentioned earlier shows that 2–18 percent of people turn to news outlets mostly *for entertainment,* 6–37 percent for *interesting views and opinions,* 4–37 percent *for in-depth reporting,* and only 30–64 percent for *news and headlines.*

35. Mullainathan and Shleifer 2005.

36. This is a similar situation to the case of advocacy in legal procedures. In their path-breaking study "Advocates," Dewatripont and Tirole (1999) argue that a legal system that relies heavily on advocates (such as the lawyer and the prosecutor) may result in biased information reported by these advocates but, on the flipside, would end up revealing more information about the case in question than what a single unbiased source (e.g., a judge) would do because the advocates need to gather extra information to be able to present a biased view.

37. Mullainathan and Shleifer 2005.

38. See Xiang and Sarvary 2007.

5   The Information Value Chain

1. See Zuckerman and Buckman 1999.

2. See Reed 2000 and Lowry 2001.

3. See Reed 2002.

4. Information in the context of decision making is not the only such context. Any digitizable content has the same feature (music, pictures, film, or software). In their classic book *Information Rules,* Shapiro and Varian (1999) discuss in detail how digital markets may differ from traditional ones.

5. See Bakos and Brynjolfsson 1999 and 2000 for a more detailed treatment of bundling in the context of competition for goods with low marginal costs.

6. See Hamm 2007.

7. In "Markets for Product Modification Information," Iyer and Soberman (2000) found, for instance, that whether the information helps to defend competitors against each other or whether it is a tool providing better means to attack each other has an effect on the optimal information-selling format. In "Buying and Selling Information under Competition," Xiang and Sarvary (2005) highlighted that exclusive selling stays beneficial even under competition if the intensity of competition is strong between customers and the information provides strong competitive advantage.

8. See "Global Financial Information Survey: Revenue, Sharing and Piracy Estimates," 2009 Report from Burton-Taylor International Consulting LLC.

9. See Bakos, Brynjolfsson, and Lichtman 1999.

6   Networks, Interfaces, and Search

1. See Read 1992 for an in-depth history of Reuters as well as Dhebar 1995. See also http://thomsonreuters.com/about/company_history/.

2. See Christensen and Overdorf 2000 and Bower and Christensen 1995 for more detail on disruptive technologies and their role in changing corporate strategy.

3. Do we pay for a Google search though? Yes we do, albeit very little, by looking at the "ads" (sponsored links) after each search, as in a standard media model.

4. Brin and Page 1998. Actually, PageRank became so famous that even *The Economist* decided to publish a user-friendly description of its concept in its Technology Quarterly; see " How Google Works," *The Economist* 372, no. 8393 (September 18, 2004): 32–34.

5. Recent interest in networks has revealed that such power law distributions are more the rule than the exception and typically apply to a large variety of networks from the network of neurons in living organisms, through collaboration networks of scientists to that of terrorist networks.

6. A famous example is Barabasi and Albert 1999. See also Barabasi's fascinating book *Linked* (2002).

7. See Katona and Sarvary 2008.

8. In 2005 there were only about twelve million blogs; see also Baker 2005. Technorati's CEO estimated that the number of blogs doubled every five and a half months with a blog added to the web roughly every second. Today, there are about 200 million independent blogs and their growth has slowed down considerably, partly because blogging has increasingly become one activity carried out on mainstream social media.

9. Mayzlin and Yoganarasimhan 2010.

10. Nass and Reeves 1996.

11. Stephenson 1992.

12. As SL denotes Second Life, RL became shorthand for "real life," because making the distinction between the two often represented a challenge for members. See Boellstorff 2008 for a detailed anthropological analysis of Second Life.

13. Actually, the numbers are somewhat confusing. At the time of writing this book, there were about one million regular SL members; however, tens of millions have tried the platform and at any moment there are about fifty thousand residents online. Membership has been steadily growing (if we discount the dip corresponding to the ban of gambling on SL), although it tapered off by the end of 2010. Linden Lab is quite profitable, earning revenues mainly from membership fees, the sale of virtual land, and transaction fees on currency exchange.

14. Thomson Reuters was one of the first companies present in SL—it had a permanent correspondent in the metaverse.

15. See Olson 2010.

16. These terms and concepts are far from new. See *The Economist*'s special report on smart systems for a good summary of the literature on the topic as well

as on current developments: "It's A Smart World," *The Economist* 397, no. 8707 (November 6, 2010): 3–4.

7   Branding Information

1. The AIDA model only applies to high-involvement, rational purchases, when the consumer actually spends some time thinking about the purchase decision. In other words, it applies to situations where (1) the purchase decision is important and (2) it serves a utilitarian purpose as opposed to an "ego-expressive" purpose. Information purchased for decision making falls into this category. AIDA has other names as well, including "hierarchy of effects," "purchase funnel," etc.

2. See details in Sarvary and Pedrero 1997.

3. See Chard and Sarvary 1997; Ofek and Sarvary 2001.

4. See Alacrawiki.com for an updated directory of business information vendors and aggregators.

8   R&D for Information and Knowledge

1. "Data, Data Everywhere: A Special Report on Managing Information," *The Economist* 394, no. 8671 (February 27, 2010). A zettabyte is 2^{70} bytes and is roughly equal to ten trillion copies of *The Economist*. Computer scientists argue that this explosion of data/information means a qualitative change for the economy and describe the last two decades as the "industrial revolution of data" and the phenomenon as "big data."

2. Ibid.

3. See Hamm 2009.

4. "It's a Smart World," A special report on smart systems, *The Economist* 397, no. 8707 (November 6, 2010): 3–20.

5. Pachube and Palantiri Systems are examples of companies providing such services.

6. Surowiecki 2005.

7. The technology platform originates from the world of software design where it was meant to help communicate software specifications within a large heterogeneous community of developers. The designer, Ward Cunningham, coined the term "Wiki" after the "wiki wiki" (meaning "quick") shuttle buses at Honolulu Airport.

8. Blumenstock 2008.

9. "The Battle for Wikipedia's Soul," Technology Quarterly, *The Economist* 386, no. 8570 (March 8, 2008): 3–4.

10. See Bohannon 2007.

11. See Bachman 2010.

12. See Stone 2010.

13. Critics also mention the fact that the original author has too much control over the content of subsequent editors. As such the system creates a barrier for the "wisdom of crowds" to operate in Knol.

14. See Berg et al. 2008.

15. See Lee and Moretti 2009. They also show that more precise polls have more effect on market prices. Their result regarding the timing of polls is somewhat counterintuitive: they find that later polls have more effect on market prices.

16. Wolfers and Zitzewitz 2004.

17. Elberse 2005.

18. Wolfers and Zitzewitz 2004.

19. Standard statistics tells us that the variance is the difference of the mean of the square and the mean squared. Therefore, from the prices on the two contracts we can estimate the variance of the variable by taking a simple difference between them.

20. Arrow et al. 2008.

21. See Akerlof and Shiller 2009.

22. Today's InnoCentive is a largely independent innovation powerhouse that brokers a broad range of R&D problems between companies and scientists. It offers cash awards for innovative solutions.

23. See Baker 2009.

24. See Goldman 2010.

25. Rheingold 2002.

9   Conclusion

1. See, for example, Pinker 1994.

2. "It's a Smart World," A special report on smart systems, *The Economist* 397, no. 8707 (November 6, 2010): 16.

References

Admati, Anat R., and Paul Pfleiderer. 1986. "A Monopolistic Market for Information." *Journal of Economic Theory* 39 (2): 400–438.

Admati, Anat R., and Paul Pfleiderer. 1988. "Selling and Trading on Information on Financial Markets." *American Economic Review, Papers and Proceedings* 78 (2): 96–103.

Admati, Anat R., and Paul Pfleiderer. 1990. "Direct and Indirect Sale of Information." *Econometrica* 58 (4): 901–928.

Ajami, Fouad. 2001. "What the Muslim World Is Watching." *New York Times Magazine* (November 18): 48.

Akerlof, George A., and Robert J. Shiller. 2009. *Animal Spirits: How Human Psychology Drives the Economy, and Why It Matters for Global Capitalism.* Princeton, NJ: University Press.

Alterman, Eric. 2003. *What Liberal Media? The Truth about Bias and the News.* New York: Basic Books.

Ariely, Dan. 2008. *Predictably Irrational: The Hidden Forces That Shape Our Decisions.* New York: HarperCollins Publishers.

Arrow, Kenneth J. 1996. "The Economics of Information: An Exposition." *Empirica* 23 (2): 119–128.

Arrow, Kenneth J., Robert Forsythe, Michael Gorham, Robert Hahn, Robin Hanson, John O. Ledyard, Saul Levmore, et al. 2008. "The Promise of Prediction Markets." *Science* 320 (5878): 877–878.

Bachman, Justin. 2010. "Q: Will Question-Asking Become Big Business?" *Bloomberg Businessweek*, no. 4191 (August 9): 38–39.

Baker, Stephen. 2005. "Looking for a Blog in a Haystock." *Business Week*, no. 3944 (July 25): 38.

Baker, Stephen. 2009. "What's a Friend Worth?" *Business Week*, no. 4133 (June 1): 32–36.

Bakos, J. Yannis, Erik Brynjolfsson, and Douglas Lichtman. 1999. "Shared Information Goods." *Journal of Law and Economics* 42 (1): 117–155.

Bakos, J. Yannis, and Erik Brynjolfsson. 1999. "Bundling Information Goods: Pricing Profits and Efficiency." *Management Science* 45 (12): 1613–1630.

Bakos, J. Yannis, and Erik Brynjolfsson. 2000. "Bundling and Competition on the Internet." *Marketing Science* 19 (1): 63–82.

Banerjee, Abhijit V. 1992. "A Simple Model of Herd Behavior." *Quarterly Journal of Economics* 3 (107): 798–817.

Barabasi, Albert L., and Reka Albert. 1999. "Emergence of Scaling in Random Networks." *Science* 286 (5439): 509–512.

Barabasi, Albert. 2002. *Linked: The New Science of Networks.* Cambridge, MA: Perseus Publishing.

Berg, Joyce, Robert Forsythe, Forest Nelson, and Thomas Rietz. 2008. "Results from a Dozen Years of Election Futures Markets Research." In *Handbook of Experimental Economics Results*, ed. Charles Plott and Vernon Smith, 742–751. Amsterdam: Elsevier.

Bikhchandani, Sushil, David Hirshleifer, and Ivo Welch. 1992. "A Theory of Fads, Fashion, Custom and Cultural Change as Information Cascades." *Journal of Political Economy* 100 (5): 992–1026.

Blumenstock, Joshua E. 2008. "Size Matters: Word Count as a Measure of Quality on Wikipedia." Poster paper on WWW 2008, April 21–25, Beijing, China.

Boellstorff, Tom. 2008. *Coming of Age in Second Life: An Anthropologist Explores the Virtually Human.* Princeton, NJ: University Press.

Bohannon, John. 2007. "Folk Wisdom for Web Sites." *ScienceNOW Daily News* (January 23). http://news.sciencemag.org/sciencenow/2007/01/23-05.html?ref=hp.

Bower, Joseph L., and M. Clayton Christensen. 1995. "Disruptive Technologies: Catching the Wave." *Harvard Business Review* 73 (1): 43–53.

Brin, Sergey, and Larry Page. 1998. "The Anatomy of a Large Scale Hypertextual Web Search Engine." *Computer Networks and ISDN Systems* 30 (1–7): 107–117.

Bulow, Jeremy I, John D. Geanakoplos, and Paul D. Klemperer. 1985. "Multimarket Oligopoly: Strategic Substitutes and Complements." *Journal of Political Economy* 93 (3): 488–511.

Chaffin, Joshua, Adrian Michaels, and Gary Silverman. 2002. "NYSE Plans Tougher Rules on Dual Roles of Analysts." *The Financial Times* (September 27): 23.

Chard, Ann Marie, and Miklos Sarvary. 1997. "Knowledge Management at Ernst & Young." Stanford Business School Case Study, S-M-291.

Chevalier, Judith, and Glenn Ellison. 1999. "Carrier Concerns of Mutual Fund Managers." *Quarterly Journal of Economics* 114 (2): 389–432.

Christen, Markus, and Miklos Sarvary. 2007. "Pricing Information: A Longitudinal Experiment." *Journal of Marketing Research* 44 (4): 46–52.

Christensen, Clayton M., and Michael Overdorf. 2000. "Meeting the Challenge of Disruptive Change." *Harvard Business Review* 78 (2): 66–76.

Cool, Karel, Chloe Harford, and Martin Oppenrieder. 2005. "Google and the Online Search Industry in 2005." INSEAD Case Study, no. 305-415-1.

Coulter, Ann. 2003. *Slander: Liberal Lies about the American Right.* New York: Three Rivers Press.

Coy, Peter. 2008. "Oil's Murky Outlook: With Reliable Data Scarce, It Is Almost Impossible to Say Where Prices Will Go." *Business Week,* no. 4085 (May 26): 23–26.

DellaVigna, Stefano, and Ethan Kaplan. 2005. "The Fox News Effect: Media Bias and Voting." Working paper, UC Berkeley.

Dewatripont, Mathias, and Jean Tirole. 1999. "Advocates." *Journal of Political Economy* 107 (1): 1–39.

Dhebar, Anirudh. 1995. "Reuters Holdings PLC 1850–1987: A (selective) History." Harvard Business School Case Study, 9-595-113.

Elberse, Anita. 2005. "How Markets Help Marketers." *Harvard Business Review* 83 (9): 32–34.

Elstein, Aaron. 2001. "As Dot-Com Era Fades, Forecasters Face Skepticism." *The Wall Street Journal,* April 17.

Emons, Winand. 1997. "Credence Goods and Fraudulent Experts." *Rand Journal of Economics* 28 (1): 107–119.

Foray, Dominique. 2006. *The Economics of Knowledge.* Cambridge, MA: MIT Press.

Franken, Al. 2003. *Lies and the Lying Liars Who Tell Them: A Fair and Balanced Look at the Right.* New York: E. P. Dutton & Co.

Gentzkow, Matthew, and Jesse M. Shapiro. 2006. "Media Bias and Reputation." *Journal of Political Economy* 114 (2): 280–316.

Gillespie, Tarleton. 2007. *Wired Shut: Copyright and the Shape of Digital Culture.* Cambridge, MA: MIT Press.

Goldberg, Bernard. 2002. *Bias: A CBS Insider Exposes How the Media Distort the News.* Washington, DC: Regency Publishing, Inc.

Goldman, Andrew. 2010. "Henry Blodget's Road from Ruin." *Bloomberg Businessweek,* no. 4187 (July 12): 58–63.

Graber, Doris A. 1984. *Processing the News: How People Tame the Information Tide.* New York: Longman Press.

Grossman, Sanford J., and Joseph E. Stiglitz. 1980. "On the Impossibility of Informationally Efficient Markets." *American Economic Review* 70 (3): 393–408.

Hamm, Steve. 2007. "These Books Write Themselves." *Business Week,* no. 4063 (December 17): 18.

Hamm, Steve. 2009. "Big Blue Goes into Analysis." *Business Week,* no. 4128 (April 27): 16–19.

Hayakawa, S. I., R. Alan Hayakawa, and Robert MacNeil. 1990. *Language in Thought and Action.* 5th ed. New York: Harcourt Brace Company.

Hong, Harrison, and Jeffrey D. Kubik. 2003. "Analyzing the Analyst: Carrier Concerns and Biased Earnings Forecasts." *Journal of Finance* 58 (1): 313–351.

Hong, Harrison, Jeffrey D. Kubik, and Amit Solomon. 2000. "Security Analysts' Carrier Concerns and Herding of Earnings Forecasts." *Rand Journal of Economics* 31 (1): 121–144.

Iyer, Ganesh, and David Soberman. 2000. "Markets for Product Modification Information." *Marketing Science* 19 (3): 203–226.

Jensen, Fred O. 1991. "Information Services." In *The AMA Handbook of Marketing for the Service Industries*, ed. Carole A. Congram and Margaret L. Friedman, 423–443. New York: AMACOM.

Kahneman, Daniel, Paul Slovic, and Amos Tversky. 1982. *Judgement under Uncertainty: Heuristics and Biases*. Cambridge, UK: Cambridge University Press.

Katona, Zsolt, and Miklos Sarvary. 2008. "Network Formation and the Structure of the Commercial World Wide Web." *Marketing Science* 27 (5): 764–778.

Klein, Daniel B., and John Majewski. 1994. "Plank Road Fever in Antebellum America: New York State Origins." *New York History* 75 (1): 39–66.

Lamont, Owen A. 2002. "Macroeconomic Forecasts and Microeconomic Forecasters." *Journal of Economic Behavior & Organization* 48 (3): 265–280.

Larréché, Jean-Claude, and David Weinstein. 1988. *INDUSTRAT™: The Strategic Industrial Marketing Simulation*. Upper Saddle River, NJ: Prentice-Hall.

Lee, David S., and Enrico Moretti. 2009. "Bayesian Learning and the Pricing of New Information: Evidence from Prediction Markets." *American Economic Review* 99 (2): 330–336.

Lichtendahl, Kenneth C., Jr., and Robert L. Winkler. 2007. "Probability Elicitation, Scoring Rules and Competition among Forecasters." *Management Science* 53 (11): 1745–1755.

Lowry, Tom. 2001. "The Bloomberg Machine." *Business Week*, no. 3729 (April 23): 76–84.

Makridakis, Spyros, Robin Hogarth, and Anil Gaba. 2009. *Dance with Chance: Making Luck Work for You*. Oxford, UK: Oneworld Publications.

Mayzlin, Dina, and Hema Yoganarasimhan. 2010. "Link to Success: How Blogs Build an Audience by Promoting Rivals." Working paper, Yale School of Management.

Michaely, Roni, and Kent L. Womack. 1999. "Conflict of Interest and the Credibility of Underwriter Analyst Recommendations." *Review of Financial Studies* 12 (4): 653–686.

Milhench, Claire. 2003. "Wall Street Banks Back in the Game." *Global Investor* 165: 27–35.

Morgan, John, and C. Phillip Stocken. 2003. "An Analysis of Stock Recommendations." *Rand Journal of Economics* 34 (1): 183–203.

Mullainathan, Sendhil, and Andrei Shleifer. 2005. "The Market for News." *American Economic Review* 95 (4): 1031–1053.

Nass, Clifford, and Byron Reeves. 1996. *The Media Equation: How People Treat Computers, Television, and New Media like Real People and Places.* Cambridge, UK: Cambridge University Press.

Ofek, Elie, and Miklos Sarvary. 2001. "Leveraging the Customer Base: Creating Competitive Advantage through Knowledge Management." *Management Science* 47 (11): 1441–1456.

Olson, Elizabeth. 2010. "Growth in Virtual Gatherings Offers Marketing Opportunities." *The New York Times* (December 1).

Ottaviani, Marco, and Peter Norman Sorensen. 2006. "The Strategy of Professional Forecasting." *Journal of Financial Economics* 81 (2): 441–466.

Pinker, Steven. 1994. *The Language Instinct.* London, UK: Penguin Books.

Popper, Margaret, Tom Lowry, Michael Arndt, Julie Forster, Andrew Park, Wendy Zellner, and Amy Barret. 2002. "Industry Outlook for 2002." *Business Week*, no. 3765 (January 14): 80–83.

Read, Donald. 1992. *The Power of News: The History of Reuters, 1849–1989.* New York: Oxford University Press.

Reed, Stanley. 2000. "Just the Yank for Reuters." *Business Week*, no. 3712 (December 18): 194.

Reed, Stanley. 2002. "No Miracle Yet at Reuters." *Business Week*, no. 3790 (July 8): 52.

Rheingold, Howard. 2002. *Smart Mobs: The Next Social Revolution.* Cambridge, MA: Perseus Publishing.

Sarvary, Miklos. 2002. "Temporal Differentiation and the Market for Second Opinions." *Journal of Marketing Research* 39 (1): 129–136.

Sarvary, Miklos, and Philip M. Parker. 1997. "Marketing Information: A Competitive Analysis." *Marketing Science* 16 (1): 24–38.

Sarvary, Miklos, and Robert Pedrero. 1997. "Marketing at Bain and Co." Stanford Business School Case Study, S-M-290.

Sasseen, Jane. 2008. "Why Moody's and S&P Still Matter." *Business Week*, no. 4092 (July 14): 32–34.

Schmidt, Robert. 2010. "Niche-Market Madoff." *Bloomberg Businessweek*, no. 4194 (September 6): 50–56.

Severin, Werner J., and James W. Tankard. 1992. *Communication Theories: Origin, Method and Uses in the Mass Media.* New York: Longman Press.

Shapiro, Carl, and Hal Varian. 1999. *Information Rules: A Strategic Guide to the Network Economy.* Boston: Harvard Business School Press.

Stephenson, Neal. 1992. *Snowcrash.* New York: Bantam Books.

Stone, Brad. 2010. "Where Silicon Valley Goes for Answers." *Bloomberg Businessweek*, no. 4200 (October 18): 44–47.

Surowiecki, James. 2005. *The Wisdom of Crowds.* New York: AnchorBooks.

Tait, Nikki. 2010. "Rating Agencies Face New EU Controls." *Financial Times* (November 5): 29.

Violino, Bob, and Rich Levin. 1997. "Analyzing the Analysts." *Information Week* (November 17).

Winkler, Robert L. 1981. "Combining Probability Distributions from Dependent Information Sources." *Management Science* 27 (4): 479–488.

Wolfers, Justin, and Eric Zitzewitz. 2004. "Prediction Markets." *Journal of Economic Perspectives* 18 (2): 107–126.

Wolinsky, Asher. 1993. "Competition in a Market for Informed Experts' Services." *Rand Journal of Economics* 24 (3): 380–398.

Xiang, Yi, and Miklos Sarvary. 2005. "Buying and Selling Information under Competition." Working paper, HKUST.

Xiang, Yi, and Miklos Sarvary. 2007. "News Consumption and Media Bias." *Marketing Science* 26 (5): 611–628.

Young, Lauren. 2008. "Getting a Second Opinion of What Ails You." *Business Week*, no. 4075 (March 17): 74.

Zuckerman, Gregory, and Rebecca Buckman. 1999. "Data Providers Face Internet Challengers." *The Wall Street Journal* (September 21): C1.

Index